CAN THE STATES AFFORD DEVOLUTION?

THE DEVOLUTION REVOLUTION

A series of Century Foundation Reports that analyzes the impact of the widespread shift of government responsibilities from the national to the state and local level.

OTHER REPORTS IN THE SERIES INCLUDE:

HAZARDOUS CROSSCURRENTS: Confronting Inequality in an Era of Devolution by **John D. Donahue**

MEDICAID AND THE STATES by **Paul Offner**

The Devolution Revolution

Can the States Afford Devolution?

The Fiscal Implications of Shifting Federal Responsibilities to State and Local Governments

Harold A. Hovey

A CENTURY FOUNDATION REPORT

1999 • The Century Foundation Press • New York

The Century Foundation, formerly the Twentieth Century Fund, sponsors and supervises timely analyses of economic policy, foreign affairs, and domestic political issues. Not-for-profit and nonpartisan, it was founded in 1919 and endowed by Edward A. Filene.

Cataloging in Publication Data

Hovey, Harold A.
    Can the states afford devolution? ; the fiscal implications of shifting federal responsibilities to state and local governments / Harold A. Hovey.
        p. cm. -- (The devolution revolution)
    Includes index.
    ISBN 0-87078-425-0
    1. Intergovernmental fiscal relations--United States.   2. Finance, Public--United States--States.   3. Local finance--United States.
I. Title.   II. Series.
HJ275.H68   1998
336.73--dc21   98–27489

Cover design and illustration: Claude Goodwin
Manufactured in the United States of America.

FOREWORD

Robert Putnam's *Making Democracy Work: Civic Traditions in Modern Italy* was one of the most important works of social science of the late twentieth century. The result of twenty-five years of study, it explored, among other things, a range of possible explanations for the dramatically differing performances of the regional government structures put in place in Italy beginning in 1970. Putnam drew many important conclusions from his study, including the widely cited observation that significant differences in civic culture, some nearly a thousand years in the making, appear to be highly correlated with the relative success or failure of these experiments in subnational government.

Since Putnam's book appeared, there have been numerous attempts to apply his approach to the American context. But I know of no evidence that it was ever discussed during the scramble to "devolve" substantial national responsibilities to the fifty states. Indeed, in the United States the diversity among the states, both real and imaginary, is more celebrated than studied. But what does it mean for the provision of public services? Certainly it is no cause for jubilation that infant mortality ranges from 10.5 per 1,000 live births in Mississippi to 5.2 in Massachusetts. Nor can the wide gulf between the highest-performing states in elementary and secondary education and the bottom tier be the result of conscious preferences for diversity.

Today, because of the movement to give the states a larger role in such programs as Medicaid, welfare, and housing, these questions have taken on a new importance. For the one sure consequence of devolution is that it will result in a wider range of administrative arrangements, means of intervention, and levels of assistance for citizens affected by these programs. Given this, the Trustees of The Century Foundation decided that serious research and analysis on the impact of devolution could be of real value to policymakers and the public. We asked Carol Kellerman, former chief of staff to Senator Charles Schumer when he was a member of Congress and now executive director of the New York City School Volunteer Program, to help us edit a series of reports on specific areas where change was under way.

In this volume, Harold A. Hovey, president of State Policy Research Inc. and the editor of its newsletters, *State Policy Reports* and *State Budget and Tax News*, explores the constraints states face in collecting taxes and financing the new responsibilities that devolution has shifted to them. He explains why some states are better prepared than others to pay for the added costs of devolution. Formerly Ohio's finance director and Illinois's budget director, Hovey has the practical experience and expertise to help us understand the wide variation in the degree of flexibility that states have in responding to new challenges. Those distinctions will be most important when the first economic recession since this decade's devolutionary swing eventually hits.

Other reports in this series include *Medicaid and the States* by Paul Offner, commissioner of health care finance for the District of Columbia; *Hazardous Crosscurrents: Confronting Inequality in an Era of Devolution* by John D. Donahue of the John F. Kennedy School of Government at Harvard University; and *Housing Policy and Devolution* by Peter Dreier, director of the public policy program at Occidental College.

We thank Hovey for his thoughtful examination of this aspect of the many issues involved in devolution.

RICHARD C. LEONE, *President*
The Century Foundation
April 1999

PREFACE

The framers of the U.S. Constitution and the Bill of Rights bequeathed a riddle in the form of the countervailing aims of the Supremacy Clause and the Tenth Amendment (reserving powers not expressly given to Washington for the states), and Americans have been trying to solve it ever since. The proper balance of power between national and state governments has been the topic of endless argument throughout our country's history as policymakers have tried to get the workings of "federalism" just right.

In the early years, states enjoyed far more legitimacy and authority than the distant national government. Some of the ambiguities of the federal system were resolved in favor of national unity by the Supreme Court's decisions in *McCulloch v. Maryland* (1816) and *Gibbons v. Ogden* (1824). Then, at mid-century, the clash between states' rights and the Union over slavery became so severe that only war could settle it. The Civil War and Reconstruction period, in which the federal government virtually occupied the defeated southern states and three new constitutional amendments were adopted, represented a vast shift of power away from state capitols.

The New Deal was another period of unprecedented central government activism, reinforced by the massive national mobilization required for World War II. The prosperity of the first postwar decades seemed to affirm the wisdom of a strong federal hand at the economic helm. Later, the struggle for civil rights echoed the rhetoric and the policy imperatives of Reconstruction. "States' rights" took on negative connotations as federal marshals marched into recalcitrant states to open schoolhouse doors to African Americans.

The power of Washington in domestic affairs reached its high-water mark in the early 1970s. The Great Society had created hundreds of new "categorical" programs to be administered locally but subject to federal policy guidelines, rules, and regulations. Federal funding for these categorical programs grew from $7.7 billion in 1962 to $41.7 billion in 1973. State and local governments were cast as the federal government's agents or subcontractors; Washington now played a role in virtually every public function in every state.

Then, two Republican presidents, under the banner of a "New Federalism," started to move the balance of power in the other direction. Nixon's new federalism was an effort to shift the Great Society's categorical grants to block grants, funded by Washington but controlled at the local level in the form of general revenue sharing. Reagan's new federalism was a far more aggressive repudiation of centralized power. Instead of providing resources while ceding control, Reagan, a former governor, sought to renounce the federal government's fiscal responsibility for large areas of public policy.

Under Reagan, more than five hundred categorical programs were consolidated into nine block grants. General revenue sharing, the hallmark of Nixon's new federalism, had disappeared by 1986. Overall, transfers from Washington to the states and cities declined, and the locus of control for block grants became state governments, not cities or local community organizations.

President Clinton, of course, came into office with the reputation and instincts of an innovative governor and had considerable sympathy with the view from the states. But before his agenda for federalism could clearly emerge, the 1994 elections brought a new cast to the 104th Congress decidedly in favor of those with experience in government at the state level: there were seventeen former governors and thirty-eight former state representatives in the Senate, and nearly half of the members of the House had previous service in state legislatures. Moreover, the number of Republican governors leapt from nineteen to thirty-one in a single election year. There was now a critical mass of fresh leaders at the state level—thirsty for authority, unified in how they would deploy it, and in sync with their congressional delegations and the new Republican majority in Washington.

These advocates of state primacy found their voice and issued a clarion call—for "devolution." Proponents of devolution promise

greater efficiency, cost savings, and innovation as power moves closer to the people, and this faith in "power to the people" is enjoying
as much of a consensus as American politics ever allows.

The tide of authority and resources is now flowing away from
Washington and toward the states. A Democratic president and members on both sides of the aisle in Congress enthusiastically supported
a law prohibiting the imposition of "unfunded mandates" on the
states; other legislation passed in the 1990s has expanded state discretion over transportation spending, drinking water standards, and
highway safety.

Then came welfare "reform," the most vivid example of the
devolution movement. A sixty-year tradition of federal responsibility for antipoverty programs was repudiated in one fell swoop,
replaced by freestanding state programs whose character and effectiveness will emerge only over time. Meanwhile, the Supreme Court
also has shown evidence of a historic tilt in favor of state authority,
throwing out such seemingly straightforward exercises of centralized
control as the requirement that local law enforcement personnel
administer a seven-day waiting period on handgun purchases.

What are the underlying causes of the devolution trend?

One is that Americans' current disenchantment with the federal
government does not seem to extend as strongly to their states and
localities. During the Depression, a 1936 Gallup poll found that 56
percent of Americans favored concentrating power in the federal government, but contemporary opinion surveys indicate that most people have little confidence in the federal government, believing states
and localities can do a better job of running most things.

Another explanation is that states and localities have been slowly but surely occupying a large and growing share of the fiscal terrain
as Washington retrenches. Federal spending on everything other than
defense, income transfers, and interest payments averaged 3.6 percent of the economy in the 1970s but has dropped back to an average
of 2.2 percent in the 1990s and was only 1.5 percent in 1997.
Meanwhile, state and community spending from revenues generated
at the local levels has continued to climb; it is now seven times as
large as the federal share.

Not surprisingly, human resources are moving in the same direction. While federal civilian employment has been declining to the
point where it is now barely 1 percent of the population, state and

local employment has reached almost 17 million—well exceeding 6 percent of the population. Statehouse politics is no longer considered minor league. Many ambitious Democrats and Republicans have dedicated themselves to careers in state and city government, and the profile of state activism has risen to the point that governors and former governors are among the most prominent, thoughtful, and articulate leaders in both major parties.

To be sure, there is something to be said for Justice Brandeis's oft-repeated description of the states as policy "laboratories" that test and winnow policy alternatives, providing the country with valuable information about what works and what does not. Indeed, there may be value in diversity itself. Since citizens and corporations differ in their priorities, the nation may be better off if there is a range of alternative packages of services, regulatory regimes, and tax burdens among the states from which voters and those with influence on policy can choose.

But the shift toward state-based government entails trade-offs and may carry fundamental and far-reaching consequences for our economy and culture that have yet to be fully recognized. The papers in this series attempt to explore those complexities, getting beyond the upbeat rhetoric of "power to the people" to examine how devolution affects real world decisions in specific areas of policy. Rather than accept without challenge the premise that authority is always better exercised at smaller levels of government, the series' authors assess the impact of devolving issues of vital importance to Americans—economic inequality, Medicaid, and housing policy.

As the world's economy becomes more integrated and more unforgivingly competitive, a fragmented American public sector may seriously hurt our prospects for narrowing economic disparities and preserving a largely middle-class society. These papers sound a clear warning of the dangers we face if the balance of power shifts too heavily in the prevailing direction.

CAROL KELLERMAN
Executive Director
New York City School Volunteer Program

CONTENTS

INTRODUCTION

For several reasons, the move to devolve federal activities and their financing to state and local governments has not been accompanied by substantial examinations of the implications of devolution for state and local budgets and tax policy. First, many state officials strongly support devolution in principle and have been reluctant to express concerns that might jeopardize devolution moves they favor. Second, there has been a widespread assumption that devolution of financial responsibilities will be combined with reductions in federal mandates that will permit reductions in state and local costs. Third, the devolution proposals seriously considered to date have featured either short-term fiscal gains for the states, as the welfare reform plan provided, or a continuation of current funding levels.

Although the subject has received little detailed attention, devolution has potential major fiscal implications for state and local governments. These effects would vary by program, by the plan of devolution being discussed, and in each individual state. Conversely, the financial circumstances and outlooks of state and local governments have substantial implications for devolution. These factors will influence what devolutionary measures are adopted and the impacts of those that are adopted. This paper covers these subjects in three chapters.

The first discusses the concept of devolution, the factors leading to interest in it, the different forms it can take, and the question of whether devolution can ever become a permanent change rather than a phase in the perpetual ebb and flow of federal-state relationships. It covers the inability of federal leaders to commit their successors to a course of action and strong tendencies for federal elected officials to devolve in principle but to centralize in day-to-day policymaking. It includes the consequences of a possible "rediscovery" of reasons for federal control, as devolutionary measures are implemented and the results become apparent.

The second chapter deals with aspects of state and local fiscal situations likely to affect the outcomes of devolution. They include: (1) interstate competition, (2) regressive tax systems, (3) possible structural deficits affecting many state and local budgets, (4) fiscal disparities resulting from mismatches of needs and resources in individual states, (5) the pressures put on state and local finances by two forces—voters and courts—over which elected officials exercise little control, and (6) vulnerabilities to economic conditions and federal policy changes.

The third describes the inherent consequences of applying the concepts of devolution described in Chapter One to the state and local fiscal circumstances described in Chapter Two. It discusses the impacts of devolution on the beneficiaries of the programs being devolved and on the finances of state and local governments, and thus on taxpayers and on the beneficiaries of programs, such as education, for which these governments have primary financial responsibility.

Two appendices contain supplemental materials collecting important background information on: (1) the current status of devolution and changes being seriously discussed in individual areas of federal activity and (2) the basic characteristics of state and local government finance. Many readers already have a background on one of the two topics, but few will be familiar with both.

1

THE ISSUE OF DEVOLUTION

INTRODUCTION: A GROWING FEDERAL PRESENCE

When they wrote the Constitution, the Founding Fathers were primarily concerned with creating a strong national government to deal with defense and foreign relations and a nation that could function as a single economic union. Like the evolution of the European Union today, the emphasis was on such issues as a common currency, presentation of common trade policy (e.g., tariffs and quotas) to other nations, and the development of a free market within the union by common systems of copyrights, patents, and courts, which would enforce contracts made anywhere in the union.

The modern government activities that are now the subject of devolution debates—supporting the poor, health care, education, care of children and the disabled, mental health, and local transportation—were all the legal responsibilities of the separate states and, as a practical matter, generally left to local governments.

Changes in technology, particularly in communications and transportation, have gradually reduced the significance of location throughout American society—eroding localism in many activities outside of government such as language and dialect, culture, production, opinions, and patterns of retailing and consumption. These changes alone would probably have caused gravitation of some government activities to higher levels of government—from municipalities to counties, from both to states, and from all three to the national government.

A complex history of political changes—encompassing a civil war, two world wars, a huge depression, a new deal, a fair deal, and a great society—resulted in an increase in the role of government relative to the private sector and in the role of the federal government relative to state and local governments. Only about a fourth of current federal spending is associated with historical national responsibilities for defense, foreign policy, and the regulation of interstate commerce. The rest relates to interest on the national debt (much of which was incurred by domestic program spending), social insurance programs like Social Security and Medicare, and support of such functions as education, welfare and social services, and transportation.

Federal taxes to support these activities now represent 15 percent of all wages and salaries for payroll taxes, about 10 percent of all personal income for personal income taxes, and nearly half of all corporate profits. Federal employees and workers in state and local government and the private sector paid through federal programs, or whose jobs depend on federal regulation, probably account for over ten million workers. Federal priorities, dollars, regulation, and procedures dominate decisions in many corners of American activity, including nursing homes, hospitals, low-income housing, welfare and social services, sewage and sanitation, and highways. These federal impacts are heavily felt in other sectors such as public schools, higher education, and law enforcement.

Unlike similar shifts to national governments in most other nations, the American shift not only retained but also fortified the role of state governments by making them the administrators of national policies in such fields as low-income health care, cash welfare, education policy, and transportation.

CONCERNS CAUSED BY THE SHIFT

This evolution caused several developments that many Americans did not like. Books can be, and have been, written on each of the criticisms. They include:

Too Much Federal Government: Many Americans believe the nation has too much government—too many bureaucrats, too much government regulation, too little private initiative, and too much government spending. They lay much of the blame on the federal doorstep. They believe their taxes are too high and correctly perceive that federal taxes account for most of what they pay.

Loss of Control and Accountability: Many Americans fear that government power is mostly too far from the governed—that national policies do not reflect local preferences and needs and that national politicians are distant from the people they govern and not effectively under the people's control.

Cookie-cutter Policies: Many Americans believe that uniform national policies are now being applied in many situations where differences in policy are appropriate to reflect different local situations and/or different local preferences. There has also been concern that federal control has stifled local and state initiative and denied the nation the benefit of experimentation by state "laboratories of democracy."

Waste and Inefficiency: At times in history, federal officials have been perceived as more honest, better qualified, fairer, and more efficient than state and local officials. However, these perceptions have changed for large groups of the population who now believe that local officials are more responsive to their needs than state officials and state officials more responsive than federal ones. A majority of Americans believe that local tax dollars are better spent than state tax dollars, and state better than federal.[1]

Huge majorities of state and local officials believe that federal mandates and financing of programs with federal grants have brought delays, red tape, paperwork, and distortions of priorities so significant that they alone account for billions of dollars annually in wasted spending or, put another way, lost opportunities to improve services without increasing costs. It is common for these officials to claim that they could produce better services with cost savings of 10–25 percent if freed from federal controls.

CONTROVERSIES OVER FEDERALISM

These criticisms of the national government are not new. Complaints about excessive federal power go back in history to the Whiskey Rebellion and the Civil War. Concern that the national government was assuming too much power underlay the debates in both Congress and the courts over the New Deal policies of President Franklin Roosevelt. Commissions to study the excessive gravitation of power over domestic policy to the federal government date back to the administration of President Dwight Eisenhower.

By many measures, the nadir of federal power was reached in the administration of President Lyndon Johnson, an era that saw the development of extensive new programs to fight poverty, provide legal services to the poor, and create new federal grant programs for central cities, education, and other functions. Since then, Americans have elected as their president candidates whose personal histories and campaign rhetoric have reflected strong antifederal themes. Both Presidents Carter and Clinton achieved their prominence as state governors and often echoed themes of state responsibilities in their pronouncements and policies. Presidents Nixon, Reagan, and Bush presented themes both of shrinking government at all levels and of shifting power away from Washington and toward state and local government. A somewhat similar shift has occurred among those elected to the U.S. Congress.

Over these presidencies, many grand themes for returning power to the states[2] have been seriously discussed. These schemes include the general revenue sharing program, special revenue sharing, block grants, the "turn-back" of responsibilities to state and local governments, and "sorting out" the federal system. In addition, many proposals for cutting federal spending, such as the Contract with America featured by Republican congressional candidates in 1994 and the policy themes of President Reagan, have focused considerable attention on federal domestic spending for such purposes as local economic development.

For complex reasons, none of these global approaches has ever been adopted. Instead federalism has continued to evolve in diverse ways with little sign of general consistency from program to program, function to function, year to year, or even in positions on the subject held by individual presidents and members of Congress.

RECENT DEVELOPMENTS

The theme of shifting (which proponents call "returning") power to states and local governments continues to appear in the statements of many national leaders. The current incarnation is often called "devolution." The term came into widespread use during and immediately after the 1994 congressional elections. Those elections brought a new Republican congressional majority into office with a strong commitment to balancing the federal budget, federal tax reduction and reform, welfare reform, and devolving power to state and local government.

During 1995, and to a lesser degree in 1996 and 1997, the Congress debated these propositions at length, became embroiled in various stalemates with President Clinton, within the majority, and between various factions in the Congress and the public.

When Congress recessed at the end of its 1997 session, few of these controversies had been resolved in any permanent way. Within individual program categories, such as education and highways, many issues of relative state and federal financial and program responsibility remained to be resolved. As described in detail in Appendix A, some of these issues may be resolved in favor of larger federal roles, some with smaller federal roles, and some may remain unresolved.

Significant changes were made between early 1995 and the end of 1997. Federal control over traditional welfare programs was sharply reduced by welfare reform legislation, which created block grants to the states and capped future federal funding. By a new law on unfunded mandates, members of Congress and the president rejected the concept of levying new responsibilities on state and local governments without corresponding federal funding and established procedures to prevent this from happening. By a compromise on the federal budget that set a seven-year path, members of Congress and the president established a federal fiscal plan calling for significant reductions in the purchasing power of future federal grants.

Many other changes were discussed in the name of devolution but not made. They included turning over increased responsibilities for low-income health care (Medicaid) to the states, new block grants in job training and other fields, and elimination of grant programs in fields ranging from legal aid and cultural activities to economic development.

Some changes were made that increased federal funding of state and local activities, notably increased spending for elementary and secondary education and need-based federal scholarships for higher education. Federal financial support of higher education was greatly increased by a new tuition tax credit and other changes in federal income tax laws. Federal control in some fields like telecommunications was increased at the expense of state and local power. Further extensions of federal power remain under discussion in such diverse fields as regulation of tobacco use and deregulation of the electric utility industry.

CONFLICTING CONCEPTS OF DEVOLUTION

The process of "devolution" does not come with an instruction manual. Like other phrases—such as "new federalism," "new localism," and "sorting out"—it denotes an approach to the perpetual issues of the division of power and financing responsibility between the federal government and state and local governments. But it is not a program or plan that can be put in the form of one or more bills and enacted by the Congress. It is a philosophy or approach that can be applied in many bills covering many programs and activities.

"Devolution" is generally used to denote some shifting of something now federal to the state and local level. But the consequences of any shift depend upon what is being shifted.

Shifting Financial Responsibility: Much of the support for devolution in the Congress has come from those who seek both federal tax reductions and a balanced federal budget and realize the enormous hurdles to achieving both, given the costs and likely growth of Social Security, Medicare, defense, and interest on the federal debt. They recognize that they are unlikely to achieve their fiscal objectives so long as the federal government retains expensive responsibilities for financing entitlement programs for the poor, local infrastructure, and substantial portions of the nation's costs for environmental protection, education, law enforcement, child welfare, transportation, and other functions.

Shifting Control over Policy: Much of the support for devolution among state and local officials and the public comes from those who seek to move government closer to the people. They seek programs better tailored to local conditions, more accountability to the public, and more responsiveness by government officials to those they serve.

Links between Finances and Policy: Discussions of federalism often include phrases suggesting a linkage between control over policy and administration and responsibility for raising money. One example is, "Those who get credit for spending money should also take the heat for raising money." There is also a widespread distrust that power over policy and responsibility for fund-raising can stay divided for a long time. This is captured by the phrase, "Power follows money." Nothing requires federal officials to maintain any linkage between control over policy and responsibility for funding.

Congress can provide money to state and local officials with only minor controls over policy. It did this in the now-repealed general revenue sharing program. It continues to do this with shared revenues from mineral extraction and timber harvesting on federal lands and with impact aid for schools serving children from federal installations such as military bases. It provides financing for Community Development Block Grants and more recently welfare reform with few controls.

Congress can also maintain controls over policy while providing little or no funding. Pollution control provides but one illustration. Federal policy decisions have driven many environmentally motivated outlays such as asbestos removal from schools, separation of storm and sanitary sewers, construction of secondary and tertiary sewage treatment plants, and extensive investments in resource recovery installations as alternatives to landfills. Federal funds have defrayed a small share, probably 5 percent or less, of the outlays for these purposes.

While using a loose definition of devolution may be adequate for some purposes, a more rigorous approach is required for description and analysis of current proposals affecting particular programs, such as education and transportation. Accordingly, Appendix A provides a taxonomy of devolution possibilities as a preface to its discussion of pending proposals for devolution of particular programs.

WILL DEVOLUTION BE A STABLE POLICY?

For devolution to achieve what its proponents contend it will, it must be enacted, appear to be a permanent change, and remain in effect for a period long enough for expected adjustments to take place. Only if these conditions are fulfilled can it reasonably be expected that devolution will produce achievements that matter, such as better schools or safer streets.

There are many reasons why interest groups, state and local elected officials, state and local employees actually delivering services, and the public receiving services may perceive any devolution to be temporary. This is particularly true for instances of devolution that involve both: (1) federal financing, such as that involved in welfare reform, plus (2) a significant reduction of federal controls.

Fears about Federal Financing: State officials have every reason to expect that the federal government's funding commitments might prove unreliable. They are aware that such commitments by any particular Congress and president cannot bind their successors. State officials have experienced the vagaries of federal funding of grants to states and are aware that their own decisions sometimes deal with state fiscal adversity by sharing it with local governments. The risks associated with future federal funding will appear particularly salient so long as federal balanced budget plans hinge, as they now do, on large cuts to as-yet-unspecified domestic discretionary programs.

The willingness and ability of federal officials to continue support of programs devolved to the states is subject to outside factors, which state officials recognize that federal officials do not fully control. The federal budget is particularly sensitive to unexpected events requiring huge outlays that might force downward adjustments in funding of grants to state and local governments. Examples are wars, widespread natural disasters, and economic risks associated with recession and with increases in interest rates that jeopardize federal budget balance.

Even without such events, state officials recognize that what appears to be a general support of state and local government finances is not a strong competitor among the claimants for limited federal dollars. The experience with the enthusiastic enactment and ultimate demise of general revenue sharing reinforces this conclusion.

Fears about Federal Control: The relinquishment of federal powers is a popular cause when stated in general terms. Specific instances of relinquishment may be achievable in the context of devolution measures that incorporate concepts of cutting (or limiting future increases in) federal outlays along with concepts of shifting control to state and local governments.

But as the memories of linked devolution of funding responsibilities and control weaken, there is reason to fear that the many arguments for greater federal controls will begin to cause federal officials to reassume many powers previously shifted to state and local officials. There is strong evidence of this happening in the context of past devolution efforts. For example, previously enacted block grants have sometimes been "re-categorized" by the Congress. Also, Congress has shown a tendency to earmark federal aid for broad purposes to include demonstration projects that are more reflective of the need for congressional log-rolling to achieve passage of federal legislation than of state and local priorities.

Also it is predictable that state and local use of devolved powers will create situations for reassertion of federal control that will appeal to future congresses and presidents. For example, fifty laboratories of democracy may create some successful policies, but uncontrolled policy experimentation will also produce blatant policy failures. Huge disparities in treatment of similarly situated beneficiaries among the states may lead to calls for federal minimum standards. Inability to report exactly how federal funds were used, a hallmark of flexible programs and little paperwork, will lead to calls for stricter federal reporting requirements.

Fears That National Benefits Will Be Temporary: Devolution will inherently help achieve many of the objectives for changes in the federal government its supporters seek. The federal government's impact on the day-to-day lives of individual Americans will be reduced. The number of federal employees will, all other things being equal, be reduced. Debates over national domestic policies and priorities will tend to shift from Washington to state capitals and to the chambers of city councils and county commissioners. And the federal budget will be smaller than it would be otherwise.

These results may not endure, however. Not only is it possible that federal control will be reasserted, as described above, but also it may be that federal savings will be lost.

Just as there are many reasons why the federal government might not adhere to a policy of relinquishing policy controls, there are many reasons why state and local officials might not adhere to a policy of accepting reduced or slow-growing federal funding for activities that are devolved. Like their federal counterparts, state governors and legislators cannot bind their elected successors. Nor will all current elected officials necessarily consider themselves as parties to some sort of a "deal" that reduces federal controls in return for state and local agreements to accept less federal funding.

Restraints of future federal costs are particularly unlikely to be effective in two situations. The first is when federal officials wish to provide additional services to the public and are willing to contribute increased resources to this end through programs using state and local governments as the delivery systems. The new child health program enacted in 1997 is an example that may soon be followed by increased federal highway spending.

The second situation will arise in the next recession, with welfare and related programs being the test. As they have in every significant recession, many state and local officials will be looking for federal fiscal relief. As they have in every significant recession, many federal officials will be looking for ways to stimulate the economy by expanded federal spending. The combination will result in consideration of federal aid expansion to eliminate what otherwise would be state-initiated cuts in cash assistance and/or programs of subsidized employment for people recently moved off welfare roles.

Even if state and local officials were somehow precluded from seeking more federal money for devolved functions, such preclusion would not bind interest groups and concerned citizens seeking additional federal spending for the poor, for education, for local roads, and for whatever other functions might be devolved to state and local governments.

COMING DEBATES OVER DEVOLUTION

Many of the federal policy debates likely over the next few years will involve issues of relative federal and state powers to control domestic policies and responsibilities to provide funding for those policies. However, these issues are unlikely to be debated and resolved in the context of legislation dealing with devolution per se.

Instead, they are likely to be debated and resolved in other contexts such as in crafting new federal highway legislation, implementing water and air quality regulations, and dealing with the consequences of implementing planned cuts in federal domestic spending. These contexts and the devolution alternatives associated with each are discussed in Appendix A.

Having devolution issues decided in many separate contexts reduces the likelihood that federal policy will reflect any consistent overriding view on devolution issues. But it does not reduce the importance of those issues.

2

REALITIES OF STATE AND LOCAL FINANCES

INTRODUCTION

This chapter discusses aspects of state and local finances relevant to proposals to rely more heavily on the states to finance government action. These aspects include: (1) competitive situations, (2) regressive taxes, (3) structural deficits and inelastic tax systems, (4) mismatches of needs and resources, (5) wide disparities in programs, (6) uncontrollable voters, (7) uncontrollable courts, (8) vulnerability to local and national recessions, and (9) vulnerability to federal aid cuts. These factors must be considered in answering the three main questions in the devolution debate:

+ Will states in the aggregate, and each individual state, have the fiscal capacity to assume devolved functions? *Can they do it?*

+ If they have the capacity to do so, will states, given their constraints, assume financing responsibilities for devolved functions? *Will they do it?*

+ If states assume these responsibilities, what consequences will follow for state taxpayers, other programs funded by states and localities and their beneficiaries, and to the futures of individual states? *What happens if they do it?*

STATE-CONTROLLED REMEDIES

Most of the nine realities of state and local finances are, to varying degrees, subject to modification by actions of the states themselves. Even when state officials cannot control a reality, such as vulnerability to business cycles, they can mitigate adverse impacts, for instance, by maintaining large reserve funds. These possibilities are described in boxes, like this one, at the end of each section.

Just because states can mitigate the impacts of some of their circumstances and policies does not mean that they will do so. The essence of devolution is to accept state decisions, particularly on such issues as how they design their tax systems and how they manage their finances.

COMPETITIVE SITUATIONS

Competitive considerations have a heavy and pervasive impact on state policies. Concerns over non-competitive tax burdens translate into pressures to keep spending, and thus taxes, low. This discourages spending in support of citizens who are perceived as contributing nothing to economic development—the poor, aged, the disabled, and those with poor educational backgrounds and/or a history of welfare dependency.

Concern over the effects of taxes on economically attractive, mobile taxpayers encourages states to minimize taxes on footloose firms, high-income households, and affluent retirees. Competition for economic development motivates huge outlays for industrial parks, sports stadiums, convention centers, highways, and other programs.

The Economic War among the States: State officials are in constant economic competition with each other. Candidates for state offices campaign on platforms including promises of enhancing their state's economic development—bringing more jobs, higher incomes, and fiscal dividends for state and local governments. They point with pride to signs of economic success such as statistics on increased employment and examples of new plants. They seek track records including not losing existing employers to the lures of other states, encouraging the growth of existing firms, and drawing new employers to their state. Their challengers leap on signs of failure such as high unemployment, plant closings and layoffs, and even the loss of professional sports teams. Business groups lobby states to eliminate signs of what they call a "poor business climate."

The Competitive Environment: Interstate competition is based in the reality of the open economy, which the U.S. Constitution guarantees to citizens of every state. It protects the rights of individuals to move to any state and enjoy the privileges of long-time residents. It permits firms from any state to sell in every state, free from tariffs and quotas, and subject to no higher taxes nor more stringent regulations than in-state firms. It permits firms to establish new plants anywhere and to abandon a state entirely for any reason—including dissatisfaction with policies of that state. Attempts by states to shelter their markets from interstate competition are consistently overturned by federal courts as violations of the commerce clause of the Constitution.

Changes in technology and the nation's economy have been increasing the impact of competitive factors on state policies and are likely to continue to do so. Reductions in the weight-to-value ratio of goods, in transportation costs, and in communications cost have liberated producers from the need to be in close proximity to customers. Whole industries—beer, potato chips, dairy products, hardware vendors, and banks—have been shifting from locally based businesses to national firms. Deregulation of public utilities is reducing the ability of state and local governments to continue policies that have imposed disproportionate taxes on them.

Competition for Jobs: There is strong evidence that the decisions of firms to locate, expand, and remain in particular states are heavily influenced by state policies, including state and local tax levels.[1] Firms planning to establish new plants or contemplating moves routinely solicit competitive offers from states. There are many examples of firms that have relocated or decided to put their new

plants in different states because of home-state taxes they consider
too high.

The impression that state policies matter is reinforced by widely
publicized studies showing that states with the lowest taxes experience
the fastest economic growth[2] and by constant public testimony and
lobbying by business groups.

Nearly all states respond to these solicitations for offers to draw
new plants, often with tax concessions tailored to the soliciting firm.
But offering such concessions only to firms that appear willing to
relocate produces criticisms of state officials for not pursuing even-
handed policies. More important, it induces all footloose firms to
consider moves if for no other reason than to induce concessions
from home states.

The impact of interstate competition has been apparent in tax
policy perceived as affecting firms' location decisions. In legislative
sessions in 1997 and in each of the two previous years, at least twenty states passed legislation to reduce business taxes in some way in
order to encourage economic development. In addition, nearly all
states allow local officials to offer concessions reducing or eliminating local taxes. Successive moves of this type suggest that taxation of
footloose firms, particularly those in manufacturing, is gradually
being reduced. State policies have been moving in the direction of
ending: (1) sales taxes on equipment and supplies used in construct-
ing new facilities, (2) property taxes on manufacturers' inventories,
machinery, and equipment, (3) for limited times, property taxes on
new plants and expansions, and (4) corporate profit taxes associated
with out-of-state sales. In addition, states are enacting special tax
concessions for particular industries such as oil and gas exploration
and production, processing of agricultural commodities, aircraft maintenance, banking, and insurance.

The adoption of business tax concessions follows a familiar pattern of competitive behavior. Typically states faring the worst in economic competition—that is, states with low per capita incomes or
slow economic growth—are the first to break new ground in reducing business taxes. Examples include property tax abatements for
new plants pioneered by the depressed southeast in the 1940s; subsidies to lure particular plants by Pennsylvania and other northeastern states two decades later; and the concept of crediting employers
with income taxes paid by employees, by Alabama and Kentucky in

the 1990s. Adoption of any new tax concession by one state quickly produces clamors in other states to match the competition.

Competition for firms extends beyond tax concessions to spending—including offers of cash grants, payment of relocation expenses, providing free land or improvements, technical assistance, and loans. States also compete for firms by providing infrastructure specific to individual facilities, like access roads, water lines, and sewers. Competitions to lure firms also often produce commitments of public resources for spending other than infrastructure, such as offering new courses at universities, vocational training and community college programs oriented to the employer's needs, and assistance in finding, recruiting, and training workers for specific plants. There has also been enormous spending of public funds for convention centers and sports stadiums largely rationalized as necessary for economic development.

All efforts to limit this competition by agreements among the states have failed. Agreements among neighboring states—such as one covering the three states in the New York City area and one covering Arkansas, Louisiana, and Mississippi—have not lasted beyond the governors who made them.

Attempts by the National Governors' Association to produce consensus have been blocked by governors of "have not" states, who have viewed them as attempts by states successful in economic development to lock in their gains. Suggestions that interstate economic development competition be limited by federal laws have met two major obstacles. First, there are serious technical problems in defining exactly what policies would be limited and how. Second, state officials have opposed such moves as a federal foot in the door to limit state policy flexibility, particularly in controlling tax policy.

Competition for Worker-households: Employed persons are not generally believed to select their state of residence for reasons related to state policies. Instead they favor where desirable jobs are available, where natural amenities (surf, ski slopes, warm weather) are available, and where ties to families and friends dictate. The exceptions are many situations in which several states fulfill the same conditions, as they do in multi-state metropolitan areas such as New York City, Chicago, Kansas City, New Orleans, Memphis, and St.

Louis. In these areas, which affect many states, there is competition for high-income residents and the retailing and service jobs and taxes that attract such residents. Because of difficulties in maintaining taxes in one part of a state different from other parts, these competitive situations affect major proportions of the total American population.

Desires to encourage residency by worker-households have been a significant factor discouraging states from adopting income taxes and from maintaining graduated rates with relatively high tax rates on high incomes.

Competition for Retiree-households: Competition is rife in tax policies affecting individuals of retirement age, who are not tied to individual states by jobs. Affluent retirees are a favorite target because they pay taxes disproportionate to the costs of serving them. Many people know retirees who have relocated to Florida, Nevada, and Texas, citing freedom from estate and income taxes as motivation along with climate.

As a result of this competition, few states now tax estates (except for taxes that can be 100 percent credited against federal estate tax liability), and states exclude larger portions of pensions and Social Security from income taxation than does the federal government. Concern that adopting income taxes would reduce their attractiveness to retirees has been a strong factor in discouraging Florida and Nevada from adopting them. Similar concerns have encouraged states to limit the progressivity of their tax systems by holding down and in some cases cutting their top-bracket income tax rates. The concessions to lure and retain the over-sixty-five group are particularly significant because the already large share of total national income and wealth controlled by this group is growing and will continue to do so as the baby boomers reach retirement ages.

A focus on economic competition discourages generous social safety net programs and encourages a search for ways to avoid policies viewed as attracting more residents dependent on public programs. Many state officials have expressed concern about becoming "welfare magnets" by implementing generous welfare policies.

Anecdotal evidence of welfare magnetism is widely believed. For example, New York City officials have long believed that the city has attracted disproportionate numbers of AIDS victims because of relatively generous cash assistance and medical care provided at public expense. For a time it was believed that Seattle was drawing homeless indigent older men nationwide because of housing and cash benefits available there. Wisconsin officials have long argued that they have drawn welfare mothers from neighboring Illinois because of their more generous benefits. Indiana officials can cite cases of elderly persons moving across the Ohio River from Kentucky in order to qualify for Medicaid nursing home care.

STATE-CONTROLLED REMEDIES

While competition will always affect tax and spending policies, those effects can be minimized by realistic appraisals of where and when differences in state policies make a difference. For example, states need not act on weak evidence of interstate migration to seek more generous social programs. If they do, they can pursue modest remedies such as taking advantage of authority in the welfare reform legislation to provide lower benefits to persons moving from low-benefit states than they provide to long-term residents.[3] Also, states can limit business tax concessions to firms that have interstate mobility, without spreading them to firms, such as retailers, inherently tied to local markets.

REGRESSIVE TAXES

Strong arguments can be made that governments should be financed by progressive taxes, that is, taxes that take a larger proportion of the income of the most affluent than of those with average incomes, and a larger proportion of the income of the middle class than of the poor. With its heavy reliance on the graduated personal income tax, the federal tax system is quite progressive. State and local taxes and charges are mostly regressive. That is, they take a larger proportion of the income of the poor than of the middle class and of the middle class than of the most affluent.

The largest single tax base supporting state and local government is consumption, typified by the general sales taxes of nearly all states and many local governments, and excise taxes on particular goods such as tobacco, gasoline, and alcoholic beverages. The reliance on consumption is regressive because consumption expenditures are larger in relation to income for the poor than for other income groups.

Regressivity is heightened because consumption of heavily taxed goods and services (e.g., tobacco, gasoline, alcoholic beverages, local telephone service) varies little with income. It is also heightened because sales taxes are typically applied to goods but not to services. The ratio of the purchase of services (e.g., decorators, domestic help, attorneys and accountants, financial services) to that of goods rises as income rises.

Another mainstay of state and local finances is the property tax. Economists debate whether the property tax is regressive or proportional, but it clearly is not progressive.

Of the three major tax bases—assets (property), consumption (sales), and income—income is the least relied upon in state and local tax systems. Unlike the federal tax, many state income taxes employ a flat rate. Others are graduated, but the top bracket rate is reached at relatively low incomes, so the tax becomes proportional for middle and higher incomes even though progressive in comparisons between low-income households and other households.

Recent changes in state tax policy have probably increased the regressivity of their tax systems. Tax reductions have been concentrated on income and property taxes. Tax increases have been concentrated on sales and excise taxes.

STATE-CONTROLLED REMEDIES

States can increase their reliance on graduated income taxes with large exemptions for low-income households or even state versions of the federal earned income credit. They can reduce reliance on sales and excise taxes and alter the bases of those taxes to include items making them more progressive (e.g., club memberships) and exclude those tending to make them regressive (e.g., food).

STRUCTURAL DEFICITS AND INELASTIC TAX SYSTEMS

Officials of many states and localities complain about structural deficits in their budgets. By this they mean that revenues from current taxes will be insufficient to pay the costs of continuing current policies, given inflation and changes in the number of public school students and other measures of the changing workloads of public programs.

If such deficits exist, states cannot absorb any costs shifted from the federal government without raising taxes or cutting existing programs. In fact, they would have to cut existing programs to avoid raising taxes, or raise taxes to maintain existing programs.

Whether structural deficits exist can be assessed by examining separately the factors driving revenues from current taxes and spending to maintain current services.[4]

Revenue Growth: The automatic growth in state and local tax revenues depends on two factors: (1) how fast the economy grows and (2) how well their tax systems capture that growth. The first factor is largely beyond the control of state officials. The second is determined by state and local decisions on the mix of revenue sources and the design of tax systems.

The mix is important because different revenue sources have a different ability to respond to economic growth. Revenues from sales taxes do not grow as fast as the economy grows because these taxes are primarily on sales of goods but not services, which are growing as a share of consumer spending. On the other hand, most state income taxes have fixed-dollar personal exemptions. As income rises, these exemptions are used up and all the growth in extra income is subject to tax. Also, in states with graduated income tax rates, additional income is taxed in higher brackets with higher rates. So income tax revenues tend to grow faster than personal income.

Design of taxes also matters. For example, some states apply sales taxes to many services while most do not. A few states and many local governments with income taxes do not have graduated rates or significant personal exemptions and deductions.

Detailed calculations by the author of the elasticity of each state's tax system show that the average state will not match personal income growth with tax revenue growth. This is the same conclusion reached by the organizations of the nation's governors, legislators, budget officers, and tax commissioners in a report, *Financing State Government in the 1990s,*[5] published in 1993. Specifically, the calculated responsiveness of state and local tax systems to economic growth, what economists call *elasticity*, is 0.96 for the nation. This means that for every growth of 10 percent in personal income, state and local tax revenues will automatically grow 9.6 percent.

The outlook for automatic growth in revenues other than taxes is not as favorable as the outlook for taxes. Many non-tax revenues do not respond automatically to inflation because they are established in fixed amounts, such as a $15.00 fee for a certified copy of a birth certificate. Federal aid under the budget compromise of 1997 is unlikely to grow as fast as personal income.[6]

Table 2.1 shows the effects of different responsiveness to economic growth on different sources of state and local revenues.[7] The data show that for the nation as a whole, current own-source revenues of state and local governments will not permit them to maintain spending that is a constant share of personal income. For example, in the eighth year, if revenue growth matched personal income growth, revenues would be 147.8 percent of base-year revenues. Actual revenues without changes in tax rates and other policies would be 138.5 percent. The shortfall is about 6.3 percent.

The table does not reflect the extent to which states and some local governments have mortgaged future revenue growth by phased tax cuts already enacted that will cause reductions in tax bases or rates in future years. Nor does it reflect self-imposed limitations on the yields

---

TABLE 2.1. PERCENTAGE INCREASE IN STATE AND LOCAL REVENUE AFTER TYPICAL EIGHT-YEAR PERIOD

CATEGORY	PERCENT CHANGE
Total General Revenue	38.5
Federal Aid	26.7
Own Source Revenue	42.1
Taxes	45.9
Non-tax Revenue	23.8
Personal Income	47.8

Source: Author calculations from a variety of sources.

of current taxes associated with the tax limitation measures in effect in some states.

Spending Growth: Complex calculations of the costs of maintaining current services for state and local governments nationwide suggest that current service spending levels can be approximated by the assumption that they will maintain the current percentage that spending represents in relation to personal income. This conclusion does not take into account certain spending increases already built into the budgets of some state and local governments. Examples are rapid increases in debt service associated with presently authorized bond issues and multi-year commitments to spending such as those made by some states for funding local schools under their state aid formulas.

Differences among States: With spending rising proportionally to personal income and revenues rising more slowly, state and local governments *in the aggregate* have mild structural deficits. So some increase in taxes would be required to maintain current services and no uncommitted revenues exist to cover costs shifted from the federal government.

The problem of structural deficits is much more severe than national averages would suggest because of wide variations among states. Some states encounter spending needs growing much faster than revenues.

For example, structural deficit issues were a hot topic in the finances of California during the early and mid-1990s. The state was experiencing sharp increases in the factors driving state spending, particularly enrollment in public schools and universities, at the same time that its economy was experiencing recession followed by sluggish economic growth.

Structural surpluses are most likely to be found in states that combine elastic tax systems with slow or no population growth overall and reductions in population in the ages for school attendance. Examples of such states are Iowa, Kansas, Minnesota, and Nebraska.

Structural deficits are to be found in states that combine inelastic tax systems, generally with no personal income tax, with above average population growth and particularly rapid growth in enrollments in public schools and universities. Examples are Florida, Tennessee, and Texas. Even with continued strong economic growth, these states must either cut spending below levels needed to maintain current services or raise taxes substantially.

STATE-CONTROLLED REMEDIES

Changes that would make state taxes less regressive also tend to make them more responsive to growth in personal income. This is particularly true for revenue-increasing changes in tax bases. Examples are eliminating the sales tax exemptions for services, ending property tax exemptions for non-poor elderly, and ending income tax exclusions and credits for retirement income.

MISMATCHES OF NEEDS AND RESOURCES

States differ in wealth, personal incomes, and indicators of the need for spending, such as the percentage of population in poverty or of school age. Often high taxpaying ability, as measured by wealth or income, is found in the same places as a low need for public services—indicated by low percentages of people in poverty and low ratios of school-age children to population.

In most countries with federal systems, national governments provide fiscal equalization assistance to reduce the impact of these disparities on lower-level governments. For example, national equalization programs are a major part of federal-state financial relations in Australia and Canada. All fifty U.S. states provide some form of school equalization assistance to deal with mismatches of tax base and enrollment in their school districts.

The United States does not provide fiscal equalization assistance. Some of its programs, such as education aid for disadvantaged pupils, tend to be equalizing. Other programs, however, are distinctly not equalizing. For example, demonstration programs and programs such as Medicaid, involving open-ended federal matching of state and local outlays, tend to provide the most assistance to those jurisdictions that have the most ability to raise funds on their own because of their strong tax bases.

As a result, per capita federal grants to state and local government are highest in Alaska and Wyoming, two states ranking in the top five of the states in any measure comparing state fiscal capacity.

Fiscal Capacity Differences: The differing abilities of states to raise revenues can be measured in a variety of ways,[8] all of which approximate the different wide disparities among states. The most appropriate way measures the tax capacity of each state by taking national averages of taxes in relation to tax bases and comparing relative tax capacity based on how much would be raised in each state given the unique characteristics of its tax base.[9] This approach is much better than relating taxes to personal income because some states obtain substantial tax revenues from the income of residents of other states, through tourism and sales from oil and gas wells and large manufacturing plants.

These estimates of tax capacity are shown in Table 2.2 (see page 26). They show a wide range of fiscal capacity differences among the states, with a high of 41 percent above average in Nevada and a low of 29 percent below average in Mississippi.

Different approaches to measurement show about the same disparities. For example, one alternative measure, known as total taxable resources, is used in a few small federal grant programs. The most recent version of it showed a range in capacity from 46 percent above average in Alaska to 28 percent below average in Mississippi.

These large differences have major implications for the states that exhibit them. For example, the spread between Nevada and Mississippi shown in Table 2.2 means that if those two states had identical tax systems—that is, if they taxed exactly the same things at the same rates—state and local revenues per capita in Nevada would be twice as high as those in Mississippi.

Comparing those states another way, if Mississippi tried to match the per capita revenues of Nevada, its taxes would have to be twice as high as Nevada's. For example, if Nevada's sales tax rate were 5 percent, the rate in Mississippi would have to be 10 percent.

The nine states with tax capacity more than 10 percent above the national average achieve this status by a combination of means, all widely recognized. Alaska and Wyoming have extensive mineral wealth to provide revenues by severance and other taxes. Connecticut and New Jersey are the top-ranked states in the nation in per capita income and thus can raise much more than the average from personal income

TABLE 2.2. TAX CAPACITY, PERCENTAGE OF NATIONAL AVERAGE, 1994

RANK	STATE	%	RANK	STATE	%
1	Nevada	140.7	26	Montana	95.9
2	Connecticut	135.7	27	Vermont	95.0
3	Alaska	131.5	28	Nebraska	94.9
4	New Jersey	128.2	29	Georgia	94.7
5	Wyoming	128.1	30	Texas	94.6
6	Hawaii	124.7	31	Missouri	93.9
7	Delaware	116.2	32	North Dakota	93.5
8	New Hampshire	113.1	33	Rhode Island	93.5
9	Massachusetts	112.5	34	Arizona	93.3
10	Colorado	110.0	35	Iowa	92.9
11	Illinois	107.5	36	Louisiana	92.0
12	Maryland	107.4	37	North Carolina	91.3
13	California	104.7	38	South Dakota	90.7
14	Virginia	104.2	39	New Mexico	90.4
15	Minnesota	103.9	40	Idaho	90.1
16	Washington	103.1	41	Tennessee	90.0
17	Michigan	101.0	42	Maine	88.7
18	New York	100.8	43	Oklahoma	86.8
19	Florida	100.2	44	South Carolina	85.6
	United States	100.0	45	Utah	85.5
20	Oregon	98.2	46	Kentucky	84.6
21	Wisconsin	96.9	47	Alabama	83.5
22	Kansas	96.9	48	Arkansas	81.0
23	Indiana	96.7	49	West Virginia	80.8
24	Ohio	96.7	50	Mississippi	70.8
25	Pennsylvania	96.6			

Source: Data taken from Robert Tannenwald, *Come the Devolution, Will States Be Able to Respond?* (Boston: Federal Reserve Bank of Boston, 1997).

taxes. To a lesser degree, Massachusetts and New Hampshire share this characteristic. Hawaii's popularity as a tourist destination gives it taxable sales per capita well above the national average and taxable property in hotels, restaurants, and vacation properties unmatched by other states. Nevada and New Jersey have large-scale legal casinos that attract taxable gambling activities plus extra revenues from sales and other taxes paid by casino visitors. Delaware has had immense success in attracting corporations, which incorporate, maintain offices-of-record, and hold large bank accounts there.

Spending Needs: Candidates, elected officials, and the media constantly compare their state's per capita overall spending and spending on particular programs with other states and national averages, implicitly assuming that spending "needs" per capita are equal from state to state. The fallacy of this approach arises because most state and local programs deal with specific services to specific populations such as educating children in public schools and state universities, providing Medicaid to low-income residents, and safety net programs for the poor. Even programs serving everyone, such as providing roads and police protection, operate differently in different circumstances. Highways cost more to construct and maintain per capita in sparsely populated rural areas than in urban areas, or in areas with rugged terrain or extreme climates. Protecting citizens against crime is more of a challenge in urban areas and densely populated states than in rural states with predominately older populations. So there is no reason to expect that spending will be, or should be, proportional to either population or, for that matter, personal income.

For example, because of fast growth and high birthrates, Utah and Idaho have much higher burdens in paying for public schools and universities. States with more mature populations, like Massachusetts and Pennsylvania, experience lower costs per capita in providing average per-pupil spending because they have low ratios of students to total population.

Welfare costs are inherently higher in Louisiana and Mississippi because larger percentages of their people live below the poverty line than in Colorado or Iowa. Police protection is inherently cheaper in New Hampshire and North Dakota because there is less crime than in some southeastern states. Per capita highway costs are over twice the national average in sparsely populated North Dakota and Wyoming.

Some states have above-average spending needs for all their activities. Mississippi is the best example. Its extraordinarily large poverty population drives a need for safety net spending. Higher-than-average proportions of young people increase the costs of education as well as law enforcement and corrections. Conversely, Connecticut has few children in relation to population, low poverty levels, relatively low crime rates, and a high population density that reduces the relative cost of roads. Table 2.3[10] summarizes the results. It is most easily understood as the answer to this question: If each state matched the national average pattern of spending in relationship to workloads such as spending per pupil, how would total spending in each state deviate from the per capita national average?

As would be expected, states like Louisiana and Mississippi show the greatest differential in overall spending needs. For example, assume that Louisiana and New Jersey had identical spending patterns, that is, they maintained the same class sizes in public schools, paid their teachers identically, and spent identical amounts per pupil on books, supplies, building maintenance, and other elements of school cost. The table is saying that to do this Louisiana would have to spend 20.4 percent per capita more on state and local services than the national average. New Jersey would spend 14.6 percent less than the average.

The huge differentials in fiscal capacity and spending needs interact with competitive factors leading to obvious state strategies. States in strong fiscal positions are capable of exploiting their strengths by maintaining low business taxes while providing above-average services, such as infrastructure and schools, that might be attractive to business. States like Mississippi can improve economic opportunities for their residents only by being attractive to private-sector employers. So their leaders have strong incentives to avoid above-average taxes and to concentrate tax burdens on individuals rather than firms. With average taxes producing below-average spending, they must also make difficult choices in spending. States like Mississippi have traditionally made these choices by concentrating spending on outlays like infrastructure and education at the expense of social welfare.

Fiscal Comfort: The Fiscal Comfort Index (see Table 2.4, page 31) is a measurement of the ease with which public officials in each state can maintain high spending and low taxes. In other words, it measures

TABLE 2.3. TAX CAPACITY, PERCENTAGE OF NATIONAL AVERAGE, 1994

RANK	STATE	%	RANK	STATE	%
1	Louisiana	20.4	26	Alaska	-1.5
2	New Mexico	17.7	27	New York	-1.7
3	Mississippi	16.1	28	Ohio	-1.7
4	Texas	11.1	29	Oregon	-2.6
5	South Dakota	10.3	30	Nevada	-3.0
6	Oklahoma	9.4	31	Minnesota	-3.4
7	Kentucky	8.8	32	Florida	-3.4
8	West Virginia	8.4	33	Washington	-4.3
9	Arkansas	7.2	34	Iowa	-4.8
10	Wyoming	6.9	35	Illinois	-4.9
11	Alabama	6.8	36	Nebraska	-5.0
12	Idaho	6.6	37	Virginia	-5.6
13	Kansas	5.0	38	Maine	-7.2
14	California	4.4	39	Colorado	-7.7
15	Arizona	4.0	40	Pennsylvania	-8.1
16	Montana	3.6	41	Wisconsin	-8.3
17	Missouri	3.6	42	Vermont	-8.4
18	Georgia	3.4	43	Maryland	-8.5
19	North Dakota	2.9	44	Rhode Island	-11.1
20	Utah	2.7	45	Connecticut	-11.3
21	South Carolina	2.0	46	Delaware	-12.6
22	Tennessee	1.8	47	New Hampshire	-12.8
23	North Carolina	1.6	48	Massachusetts	-13.3
24	Indiana	0.7	49	Hawaii	-14.5
25	Michigan	0.4	50	New Jersey	-14.6
	United States	0.0			

Source: State Policy Reports 16, no. 5 (1998).

the relative advantages and disadvantages of individual states in financing and providing the services of state and local governments.

Mathematically, the Comfort Index is the Index of Fiscal Capacity of each state divided by its Index of Spending Need.[11] The index values are percentages of a national average, which is set at 100. For example, Table 2.4 indicates that Connecticut is 53 percent better off than the national average while Mississippi is 39 percent worse off.

The contrast between these extremes is like a very short person and a very tall one standing in a room and being challenged to jump to touch the ceiling. The tall person has less distance to jump and, with longer legs and equal leg strength, more capacity to jump.

STATE-CONTROLLED REMEDIES

Individual states cannot solve situations in which their limited tax bases make it difficult to handle their above-average needs for services.

WIDE DISPARITIES IN PROGRAMS

Because of disparities in fiscal capacity and needs among the states and because of other factors such as political cultures, there are massive variations among states in safety net programs.[12] Typical family welfare (AFDC) payments in FY 1995 ranged from $120 a month for a family of three to $923. In FY 1996, one state provided more than $2,000 in annual state-funded supplements to federal Supplemental Security Income benefits while nine provided no supplements at all. Eight states do not have any form of general assistance—cash assistance available to persons not eligible for federal categorical programs—nine states have programs in some counties and not in

TABLE 2.4. FISCAL COMFORT INDEX, FY 1994, PERCENTAGE DIFFERENCE FROM THE NATIONAL AVERAGE

RANK	STATE	%	RANK	STATE	%
1	Connecticut	153	26	Ohio	98
2	New Jersey	150	27	Iowa	98
3	Hawaii	146	28	Indiana	96
4	Nevada	145	29	Maine	96
5	Alaska	133	30	Montana	93
6	Delaware	133	31	Kansas	92
7	Massachusetts	130	32	Georgia	92
8	New Hampshire	130	33	North Dakota	91
9	Wyoming	120	34	Missouri	91
10	Colorado	119	35	North Carolina	90
11	Maryland	117	36	Arizona	90
12	Illinois	113	37	Tennessee	88
13	Virginia	110	38	Texas	85
14	Washington	108	39	Idaho	85
15	Minnesota	108	40	South Carolina	84
16	Wisconsin	106	41	Utah	83
17	Rhode Island	105	42	South Dakota	82
18	Pennsylvania	105	43	Oklahoma	79
19	Vermont	104	44	Alabama	78
20	Florida	104	45	Kentucky	78
21	New York	103	46	New Mexico	77
22	Oregon	101	47	Louisiana	76
23	Michigan	101	48	Arkansas	76
24	California	100	49	West Virginia	75
	United States	100	50	Mississippi	61
25	Nebraska	100			

Source: Author calculations from various sources.

others, and the remaining thirty-three states have statewide programs. These have widely varying eligibility criteria and benefits.

Total Medicaid spending in 1994 varied from over $4,000 per
low-income person in five states to under $1,300 in about ten states.
Spending on acute care per low income person was over $1,800 in
three states and less than $700 in five. Spending on long-term care
shows even more disparity. Similar differences appear in many other
safety net programs.

STATE-CONTROLLED REMEDIES

Officials of states with low benefit levels do not necessarily view low
levels as a problem needing solution. Officials of states with higher benefit levels may view high levels as a problem if benefits are
perceived as causing in-migration of welfare recipients or excessive
tax burdens. So state-controlled remedies to benefit disparities work
in the direction of leveling down, not leveling up.

UNCONTROLLABLE VOTERS

With devolution, the federal policy takes state institutions as it finds
them—including laws established by voter decisions and by court
decisions (see the next section). This situation is quite different from
the one prevailing when the federal government dictates state policies
by mandates, conditions attached to federal grants, and preemptive
federal laws.[13] Such federal action controls state policies, not just
state laws passed by legislatures and administrative regulations, but
also provisions of state constitutions, decisions of state courts, and
decisions of voters made by voter-initiative. The difference is important because finances of states and local governments are significantly affected by voter-initiated legislation and spending demands
originating in state court systems. These effects vary from almost
none in some states to major limits on state fiscal capacity in others.

Direct Democracy: In most states, voters affect policy only indirectly through their choice of elected officials and by their votes to approve or disapprove constitutional amendments placed on the ballot at the initiative of legislators. However, the "direct democracy" movement of the early twentieth century provides more substantial controls for voters in nearly half the states. In those states, voters can act to put decisions to a popular vote by obtaining a stipulated number of voter signatures on petitions. With sufficient signatures, voters can act directly to: (1) recall persons previously elected to office even though they have not completed their terms, (2) refer measures passed by the legislature to a popular vote, making the measures inoperative until approved by a majority of voters, and (3) initiate legislation on their own.

Initiative measures have had major impacts on the finances of states where initiatives are allowed. California is the longest running example. A voter initiative (Proposition 13) radically changed state and local finances by rolling back property taxes and ending the automatic link between market values and values assessed for property tax purposes. Another initiative (the Gann Amendment) places limits on state taxes and spending. It has parallels in other states such as the Hancock Amendment in Missouri and the Headly Amendment in Michigan. Also in California, Proposition 98 has significantly altered the distribution of state spending by creating a constitutionally determined minimum allocation of state funds to school aid. Initiatives in other states have resulted in limits on taxes and spending, prohibitions against tax increases without voter approval, and various limitations on legislatures' ability to adopt particular taxes.

These initiatives and the potential for additional ones have influenced the ability and willingness of state elected officials to provide funding for particular programs—particularly the programs for low-income populations that are involved in much of the discussion of federal devolution. The combination of limits on state spending and the earmarking of spending for education have forced California officials to abandon past practices of indexing cash assistance payments to reflect inflation and encouraged general austerity in spending for welfare and social services. A 1990 initiative to roll back property taxes with lost school revenue to be replaced by the state, supplemented by a more recent initiative rolling back property taxes even further, is a large part of the explanation of why Oregon's ambitious plans to extend state-financed health care to the poor have largely not been implemented.

Referral procedures also have impacts. For example, early in the 1990s the legislature in North Dakota adopted several tax increases designed to provide additional funding for public schools as well as cover the rising costs of state programs, particularly corrections and Medicaid. By petition, a group of voters forced these decisions to a popular vote. The state's voters rejected the increases.

Tax and Spending Limits: Tax and spending limits have been put into the constitutions of some states by voter initiative and into the constitutions of others by legislative-sponsored amendments designed to head off more serious restrictions in pending initiative measures. These limits take many forms, but all restrict the ability of current elected officials to increase state services and state aid to local governments even when they have the money to do so without raising taxes.

The least restrictive forms limit state taxes and/or spending to a fixed share of personal income. These guarantee that government roles in the economy never get larger, but do not require government to shrink. They can prove extremely restrictive in times when most people agree government spending should expand, as in the post-World War II baby boom when government needed to expand because such a large percentage of the population needed teachers and school buildings.

Some limits are more restrictive than fixed shares of personal income. They typically limit growth rates from a base period to the sum of the growth rates in (1) population and (2) price levels, or inflation. Over time, these limits mean that spending must shrink as a percentage of personal income because personal income is growing by the sum of (1) population, (2) price levels, and (3) real per capita economic growth resulting from national productivity improvements.

Over long periods, the more restrictive limits require contractions of government services. They provide for inflation-matching pay increases for government employees while private employees are receiving increases reflecting both inflation and about a 1.5 percent annual real increase in compensation.

Followed for, say, ten years, this policy would mean that compensation of sanitation workers, jail and prison guards, and teachers would be 15 percent lower at the end of the period relative to private sector workers. Besides proving unacceptable to the public workers, such a policy would create major problems for governments seeking to fill positions with qualified candidates.

The philosophy underlying voter-imposed limits on state taxes and spending combined with a desire to limit property taxes has encouraged states to adopt tax and/or spending limits on local governments. The limits take many forms including limiting the rate of increase in spending, preventing the assessed value of property from rising as fast as market value, and restricting the local tax rate. Without increases in state aid to make up the lost revenues, these limits frequently prevent local spending from growing proportionally to personal income.

UNCONTROLLABLE COURTS

Just as the U.S. Supreme Court is the final arbiter of what the U.S. Constitution requires, the state supreme courts are final arbiters of what state constitutions require. Particularly in states that elect their supreme court justices, some state courts have often interpreted state constitutions to require additional state and local spending.

Some decisions have come through interpretations of protections of rights in state constitutions that parallel interpretations of similar provisions in the Bill of Rights in the U.S. Constitution. Such decisions have covered issues such as standards for state prisoners, defendants' right to counsel, and programs provided in state institutions for the developmentally disabled and mentally ill.

Over the past two decades, there has been considerable litigation over school finance. The U.S. Supreme Court has concluded that the federal Constitution does not require minimum standards for elementary and secondary education programs (and thus costs) and that differences in per-pupil tax bases among school districts do not violate rights protected by the Constitution.

Most state supreme courts have been confronted with the same questions under provisions of state constitutions. About half of them have concluded that their state's constitution requires more equalization in school finance than was being provided by the combination of the state's arrangements for local financing of schools and state equalization aid. A few state courts have concluded that equality in education was insufficient, that the state must guarantee a minimum or adequate standard of education. These decisions are having a massive impact on state finances. Like the guarantees of minimum education funding adopted by

California voters, their impact has been to reduce state flexibility to provide resources for welfare, health, and social service programs.

STATE-CONTROLLED REMEDIES

From some perspectives, voter initiatives that restrict access to the full array of taxes to support government programs and state court mandates of spending that may not comport with the priorities of state-elected officials are independent factors that must be taken into account in considering the impacts of devolution. From another perspective, actions that limit a state's ability to handle devolved and regular fiscal challenges are "self-inflicted" by actions in individual states. From this perspective, controlling state constitutional law and influencing voter decisions are challenges that should be met within individual states. If the programs devolved to the individual states are truly matters primarily of state and local impact, self-imposed limitations on state ability to fund these programs are of no national significance.

VULNERABILITY TO LOCAL AND NATIONAL RECESSIONS

Historically state government finances have followed patterns closely associated with business cycles. In times of prosperity, revenues from sales, income, and other taxes grow rapidly. At the same time, some spending needs, such as those for safety net programs, are reduced because of lower unemployment. Although there is some building of balances for rainy days in these situations, states have typically used this prosperity to cut their taxes and to increase spending in ways (e.g., local aid and employee pay increases) that are not easily reversed.

Recession typically causes such substantial shortfalls in revenues and increases in spending that states cannot sustain their budget patterns and meet their balanced budget requirements. As a result, recessions typically see both cutbacks in spending and increases in taxes to restore states to solvency.

The federal government is similarly vulnerable, but it is not constrained by balanced budget requirements. So increases in spending and reductions in revenue associated with recession are automatically handled by increasing federal borrowing. The resulting deficit is acceptable in federal fiscal policy and actually sought, as what economists call an "automatic stabilizer," contributing to "counter-cyclical" economic policy. Reduced tax revenues and increased outlays put additional purchasing power in the private economy, helping to increase private sector purchasing power to lead the nation out of recession.

In many post-World War II recessions, these automatic effects have been viewed as insufficient by federal policymakers. As a further remedy, policymakers have opted for temporary tax cuts and/or increasing federal outlays for such purposes as extending Unemployment Compensation benefits, providing public sector jobs primarily by extra aid to state and local government, and stimulating federal, state, and local government construction outlays.

State and local governments behave in a "pro-cyclical" fashion, adding to the severity of recession. Their automatic reductions in revenue and increases in spending trigger fiscal crises because they put these governments in violation of their balanced budget requirements. To restore balance, they must increase taxes and reduce spending.[14] In such fiscal crises, states often resort to drastic measures such as across-the-board spending cuts.

A program that is devolved will shift from having spending protected and perhaps expanded in recession to having spending cut in recession. This will trigger understandable pressures on the federal government to provide extra aid to state governments to maintain and perhaps augment spending on such programs—such as by continuing cash assistance (welfare) payments that would otherwise be reduced by the states and by creating additional jobs under workfare programs.

The impact of national recessions on individual state economies and thus on state finances is quite uneven. A classic business cycle downturn concentrates the slowdown on private sector employment in manufacturing, particularly production of producer goods (e.g., machine tools and construction equipment) and of consumer durable goods such as vehicles, furniture, and appliances. These industries are disproportionately concentrated in the industrial Midwest and increasingly in some southern states such as the Carolinas. The next nationwide recession might be concentrated in some other industry, such as financial services. Such a recession would have its effects concentrated in New York City (and thus in Connecticut, New Jersey, and New York) and to a lesser degree in other East Coast states, particularly Massachusetts and North Carolina.

Individual states can undergo recessions even in the midst of national prosperity. During the late 1990s, Hawaii was an example because of its vulnerability to trends in tourism and the poor performance of the California, and especially the Japanese, economy. Localized recessions have occurred throughout history in states heavily reliant on a single manufacturing industry, such as aircraft manufacturing in Washington and automobile manufacturing in Michigan. Localized recessions are common in states whose economies are heavily dependent on variations in the price of commodities traded in world markets. The oil bust of the mid-1980s and the boom and bust cycles in Western mining states over the past century provide examples.

These localized recessions have the same fiscal effects on the affected states as national recession has on most states. As a result, they would likely produce the same fiscal crises and the same cutbacks in state spending, including welfare and any other programs devolved to the state level. However, the likely federal response would differ. Without a national recession, there is no macroeconomic argument for expanded federal support to maintain spending. Because the affected states enjoy windfalls from booms and keep the proceeds as well as suffer the shortfalls from busts, there historically has been little support among presidents and members of Congress for federal assistance to deal with their effects on state finances.

STATE-CONTROLLED REMEDIES

The vulnerability of state governments to fiscal crises associated with national and local recessions is determined by state policies. States can reduce this vulnerability by resisting the temptation to over-commit to tax cuts and permanent spending increases when finances are strong and by maintaining larger reserves for when their economies weaken.

VULNERABILITY TO FEDERAL AID CUTS

Federal aid accounts for approximately 23 percent of state and local general revenue, more revenue than any single tax source including property and sales taxes. Some of this money truly supplements state and local funding, adding to whatever these governments would otherwise spend. Loss of this aid to budget cuts may have a significant impact on the beneficiaries of the programs, but little impact on state and local budgets because the change in federal aid can flow through nearly dollar-per-dollar to a reduction of benefits.

However, much federal aid contributes to state and local finances in a way similar to how the income of the lesser earner in a two-income household contributes to household finances. Although the extra income may be separated in household accounts and used for specific spending, such as the food budget or mortgage payments, the purchasing power is an integral part of household finances. Major reductions of the income result in general readjustments of living standards, with impacts on all discretionary spending.

Devolution gives this interaction of federal aid and state and local finances new significance. The ability and willingness of state and local officials to support devolved functions will be affected by decisions on federal aid not only for the devolved function but also for other federal programs.

STATE-CONTROLLED REMEDIES

States can reduce the short-term impact of federal aid cuts by tapping any reserves maintained to hedge against recession. They cannot reduce the long-term effects on their finances.

CONCLUSION:
CAN STATES PAY FOR DEVOLVED FUNCTIONS?

The fiscal disabilities and problems of states described in this chapter are real. They reflect the practices and preferences of federal, state, and local officials now incorporated in the current patterns of federal aid, in the allocation of power and responsibilities between state and local governments, in their tax systems, and in their spending patterns. These are the realities that determine what will actually happen if functions are devolved.

Could states make their situations different if they chose to do so in order to meet the challenges of devolution or for other reasons? To some degree, as noted in the boxes in each section of this chapter, the answer is no. They cannot control federal aid decisions, nor the national economy, nor have much impact on their own economic and demographic circumstances.

But in many respects, as also suggested by the boxes, the answer is yes. Even if they cannot control all of their circumstances, states can often mitigate their effects. In other cases, state officials and voters are clearly in charge. For example, they can deal with structural deficits by raising certain taxes, and they can relax the constraints they impose on their finances by constitutional limits on taxes and spending. But the fact that they can do these things does not mean that they will. Nor does it necessarily mean they should. It certainly doesn't mean that national policies on devolution can be made on the assumption that they will.

STATE-CONTROLLED REMEDIES, FUNDING DEVOLVED PROGRAMS

In broad terms, governments in the United States have vast unused fiscal capacity. By raising tax levels to those of many other industrial nations or by returning to levels the United States has reached in wartime, these governments could plausibly increase taxes and spending by as much as 11 percent of the total national personal income. If all of these increases were made by state and local governments, they could double their tax-financed spending. Whether doing so is appropriate public policy is a different question. Many argue that government already takes too large a share of the nation's purchasing power.

People who want a state to spend more on a particular program are often confronted with the argument that the state "cannot afford" to do what they suggest. This is never strictly true. States can always afford to do more of something by doing less of something they already do. States can also raise more money by raising taxes and fees. But the argument that states cannot afford something are persuasive enough so that proponents of doing something new often feel compelled to suggest specific ways in which states could save money or raise more money.

The lists of these ways that could be suggested for making devolution affordable are no different from the lists associated with making other cost-increasing policies affordable. Furthermore, just because an advocate of a particular increase in state spending proposes an appealing idea for increasing state revenues or cutting spending does not mean it is logical or necessary for the freed resources to be applied to that advocate's particular spending proposal. Nor is it obvious that the appealing ideas should result in any spending increases rather than tax cuts.

So the question of whether the states can "afford" devolution is no different from other questions like whether the states can afford longer school days and school years, higher teacher salaries, more university scholarships, universal health care insurance for the poor, higher welfare payments, or more and better parks. Answering the question for any of these involves dissertations on state budget-cutting and state tax-raising. Many people have ideas about the content of such a dissertation. The author, who has spent a lifetime dealing with these issues, certainly does.

Ways to save money in state budgets to make room for new spending are constantly being offered by interest groups and candidates. They start with ending "waste, fraud, and abuse." They then move to "cutting low priority programs" and "cutting the fat" from the budgets. Neither the author nor readers can confidently dismiss these suggestions; both probably have their own lists of cuts that should be made. But these lists are unlikely to be identical. What is "fat" to one observer is "bone" to another.

A similar situation prevails for ways in which governments can gain more revenues. State and local governments can raise more money in many ways, each way probably appealing to some readers and repulsive to others. Examples: (1) higher taxes on products deemed to be harmful, such as alcoholic beverages, tobacco products, and gas-guzzling vehicles; (2) leveling the economic playing field by higher taxes on inherited wealth and "unearned income" such as interest and dividends; (3) user charges covering full costs of providing highways and roads, higher education, campsites, stocking fish, roads and schools for new housing developments, and more; (4) closing "loopholes" in sales taxes by taxing services and goods sales presently exempt; and (5) closing "loopholes" in income taxes by ending tax shelters and taxing all retirement income. This list could be expanded from a sentence to a paragraph, a paragraph to a chapter, and a chapter to a book.

There are many federal actions that would assist states in dealing with the fiscal consequences of devolution. If the federal government would close its own "tax gap"—taxable income that escapes detection of the IRS—the states would gain billions in additional revenue because their income tax enforcement piggybacks on federal enforcement. If the Congress would pass legislation granting states jurisdiction to tax mail order sales, sales tax leakage of at least a billion a year would be ended. If the Congress would pass a minimum national corporate income tax equivalent to the floor that federal policies now provide for estate taxes, states would no longer engage in the competitive erosion of their own tax bases due to interstate competition.

So there is no shortage of ideas to make devolution affordable. There are arguments that each of these ideas has merit, with or without devolution. But there are also arguments that each of these ideas is wrongheaded, with or without devolution. Devolution, which forces more spending pressure to the state and local level, would, no doubt, cause these ideas to receive more attention—but no more and no less attention than would be caused by any other situation of equivalent fiscal impact, such as a revenue shortfall associated with recession or spending pressures caused by new unfunded mandates.

3

THE CONSEQUENCES OF DEVOLUTION

NEW CHALLENGES AND OLD PROGRAMS

Discussion of devolution concerns "old" programs designed to deal with "old" problems still extant. However, the philosophy of devolution has implications for establishing and funding "new" programs to meet "new" problems and newly appreciated needs for government action. If devolution is the solution for many old programs, the philosophy argues that state and local, not federal, initiatives should be relied upon to deal with new problems and programs.

There is already a substantial list of popular possibilities for expanding government services. More will probably appear as the years go by. Examples from the current list include:

- *Health Care:* Both the size of the population without health insurance and the proportion of families without coverage are likely to grow as an increasing number of jobs are with firms that do not offer coverage or offer it only at prices many people cannot afford.

- *Early Childhood Programs:* Recent research suggests that the period from birth to age three is more important in human development

than previously believed. Little government spending is currently directed toward child development at these ages.

♦   *Governments as Parents:* Current policies lead to a large and
    growing number of children becoming wards of state and local
    governments. That is, government employees or contractors
    become legally responsible for their support, supervision, and
    decisions such as consenting to medical procedures. These situa-
    tions arise when children are abandoned or taken from their par-
    ents because of child abuse and when older juveniles are placed
    under state supervision because of criminal violations. Criticism
    of the resulting arrangements—perpetual foster-care and juve-
    nile institutions—is leading to more interest in arrangements such
    as subsidized adoptions, with potential large increases in public
    costs.

♦   *Education Quality and Intensity:* Many Americans support a
    list of expensive ideas that would make American public schools
    more like those of Europe and Japan, including substantial
    increases in the length of the school day and the school year.

♦   *Transportation:* The nation's Interstate System is little changed
    from its original design in the 1950s despite population and traf-
    fic growth and major shifts of population to locations not cov-
    ered in the original plan. In rapidly growing states, investments
    in arterial roads have not matched increased traffic, while in
    older states, renovation of various transportation systems, tran-
    sit as well as roads, is becoming an increasingly pressing need.

The impacts of devolution, particularly the demands they could
place on state and local finances, include the responsibility for dealing with situations like those above.

Federal policy already presumes that state and local governments
will be responsible for meeting these demands without increasing federal financial participation. The federal budget compromise of 1997
includes projections of future federal outlays for seven years. Those
projections presume no new federal programs, no expansion of the
scope of existing programs, and reduced federal support of federal
programs already in existence.

EVALUATING DEVOLUTION

Defining Devolution Precisely: Because the concept of devolution covers a range of situations,[1] and can be applied in different ways from program to program, discussion of its consequences often lacks focus. Critics can claim evils that proponents can assert are not inherent in the plans they favor. Proponents can claim benefits the critics claim are not inherent in the plans they attack.

The lack of a precise model makes rigorous analysis of fiscal effects impossible. Indeed, an analysis of concepts of devolution in Appendix A shows situations in which something that can be called devolution would not provide any fiscal challenges for state and local government. The proposals for new federal highway legislation to be considered by the Congress in 1998 are an example. They would offer new flexibility to state and local officials while increasing federal support of highway construction. The effect of such changes would clearly be to improve state fiscal situations.

Such proposals have great practical importance, but do not raise significant fiscal questions related only to devolution proposals with specific characteristics, such as those that appeared in the federal welfare reform legislation. The analysis of the fiscal effects of devolution in this chapter deals only with devolution that exhibits these features:

- *Federal Savings:* The projected federal outlays for the activity are lower than the outlays from a continuation of current federal policies.

- *No "Shift and Shaft":* The federal government does not mandate that state and local governments continue to implement the former federal programs.

- *Increased Flexibility:* State and local governments are given more freedom to reduce spending and change program characteristics than they were previously allowed.

Non-fiscal Dimensions: Some critics of devolution have objections unrelated to fiscal effects. It can be argued, for example, that compared with state and local governments, the federal government is (1) less likely to discriminate based on race, sex, and national origin; (2) more efficient; (3) less dominated by special interest groups such as business generally or business interests prominent in particular states such as gambling, ranching, or manufacturing; and/or (4) more likely to adopt sound policies. These arguments are beyond the scope of this report.[2] Some supporters of devolution offer arguments in its support that are the exact opposite of those listed above. Those too are beyond the scope of this report.

Implementation Details: Many objections to proposals to devolve federal programs are unique to the particular proposal for federal action that is the subject of attention. Examples are concerns that the proposal has an inequitable formula for distribution among states, does not provide ample opportunity for evaluation, or has minimum standards that are inadequate. Such objections can be overcome by changes in the design of the proposed federal action. These concerns and the program features that could be designed to meet them are unique to individual devolution proposals and are *not* covered in this report.

Cascading, Interactive Effects: Devolution simultaneously provides states with: increased financial responsibility and increased program control. How they respond to each interacts with how they respond to the other. However, the forces put in motion by devolution are best understood by considering the effects separately as is done below.

INCREASED FISCAL PRESSURES ON STATE AND LOCAL GOVERNMENT

If every characteristic of devolved programs remained the same, federal savings from devolution would have flip sides. Every dollar saved in the federal budget would have to be matched by an extra dollar of fiscal burdens on state and local governments. The result would be the same as what happens to a family budget when some uncontrollable factor increases costs, such as an increase in monthly payments on an adjustable rate mortgage. Economists call this an *income effect*.

States and households have two options for adjusting to the higher costs. One is to maintain their spending patterns by increasing their revenues—taking a second job or more overtime for a household and raising fees or taxes for a state. The other is to cut enough of their other spending to make room for the new costs they are experiencing.

POSSIBLE "SAVINGS" FROM DEVOLUTION

Neither cutting spending nor raising taxes is particularly appealing to state and local officials. So the first question arising from devolution is whether state governments need to maintain the same services, delivered the same way, with the same costs as when the program was driven by federal policy. The initial presumption is likely to be no.

State support for devolution is largely based on the premise that states can use money better if freed of restrictive and prescriptive federal rules and paperwork. State officials often assert that they could deliver the same benefits at lower cost if they had more control. So each instance of devolution provides an opportunity to turn these assertions into reality by reducing costs with no discernible impact on services being provided.

The extent of such savings depends on what is being devolved and what federal restrictions and mandates remain applicable after devolution.

Cost Reduction: Savings arise when previous federal policy has dictated that states pay higher prices than states pay when using their own funds. There are many examples of such situations. For example, when federal funds are used for construction, federal policy dictates that construction workers be paid the "prevailing wage." In practice, this means union rates that are higher than most states pay for construction when spending their own funds. Another example comes from the more complex provisions on labor issues built into some federal programs, such as those affecting the use of part-time workers in transit systems. Yet another example comes from federal policies that affect prices paid to health care providers.[3] Certain cross-cutting federal policies also tend to increase state and local costs in all programs affected by them. Examples are preferences for minority contractors and uniform policies regarding paying relocation costs of those affected by government land purchases.[4]

Another category of savings is linked with elimination of "paperwork" associated with federal programs, including all costs connected with applying for assistance, providing progress reports, maintaining required statistics, and conducting mandated evaluations.

Realization of these savings is not automatic. Some states impose constraints on their own activities, such as prevailing wage requirements, at least as costly as the ones the federal government requires. Left to their own devices, some states would not follow procedures, such as competitive bidding for certain types of contracts, which many people believe are cost-decreasing. In certain fields, such as highway contracting, many people believe that federal requirements have sharply reduced corruption that would otherwise exist.

Reducing or Eliminating Low-priority Programs: States may use flexibility to redirect resources to reduce activity, and thus spending, in particular programs. This is best viewed as simple budget cutting made possible by new flexibility, but some people like to call the results "savings."

For example, state and local officials have long complained that federal substance abuse money has been inappropriately earmarked to certain types of substance abuse, specifically drug abuse and alcoholism. In some situations, such as that of New York City, drug abuse is considered a huge and pervasive problem and alcoholism a less serious concern. In some situations, such as that of South Dakota, alcoholism is considered a huge and pervasive problem and drug abuse a less serious concern.

Allowing flexibility rather than earmarking separately for alcoholism and substance abuse is likely to result in a reordering of spending on both situations. In this example, reductions in drug abuse spending in South Dakota could be characterized as savings. But unlike savings associated with reductions in paperwork and in prices paid for government purchases, these "savings" are associated with reduced treatment of South Dakota drug abusers.

Finding Better Ways to Achieve Objectives: If state and local officials have the freedom to follow their own preferences in achieving particular objectives, they will not necessarily implement the strategies and programs formerly administered by the federal government. For example, some states might decide that substance abuse problems have causes not addressed by traditional substance abuse programs and try to reduce substance abuse by spending more federal money differently—on mental health, perhaps.

Many examples have already appeared in implementing welfare reform. To attempt to reduce welfare dependency and costs, some states are now continuing substantial subsidies for medical care and subsidized day care to former welfare recipients now holding jobs. Some are continuing cash assistance to supplement wages of full-time workers and offering subsidies to employers. Many of these policies represent spending that would not have been eligible for federal matching funds under the old (AFDC) program.

Such changes in strategies for achieving objectives may result in savings or they may result in higher costs. That there will be differences of opinion on such issues is amply demonstrated by state responses to welfare reform. Some states have opted to increase spending on former welfare recipients substantially but others have opted not to do so.

Rejecting Objectives: State and local officials may not share certain federal policy objectives and therefore could reap immediate "savings" from redirecting any flexible federal assistance away from achieving those objectives.

Housing, an area where various proposals for devolution have been considered and dropped, is a good example. Probably everyone would agree that raising the standard of living of the poor would be a good idea. Given higher incomes and a choice in how to spend them, poor persons would undoubtedly use a portion of their increased purchasing power to improve their housing. To cause them to spend more than this on housing, government would have to subsidize housing consumption directly, not just improve the incomes of the poor.

State officials, with sparse exceptions, have not viewed it as desirable or appropriate to deal with housing as a separate objective of policies for dealing with low incomes. Most state and local governments spend none of their tax money for subsidized housing. Their programs are 100 percent funded by federal resources, such as the value of tax-exempt borrowing used by state housing agencies and federal subsidies to local public housing authorities.

Federal officials have for fifty years pursued an objective of decent housing for every American and spend billions annually in pursuit of that objective. Finding the resultant policies expensive, fraught with unintended consequences, scandal-ridden, and largely ineffective in achieving their goals, for twenty years federal officials have sought the greater participation of state and local governments in housing policies. Little devolution has been achieved because state and local officials have shown negligible interest in committing their own tax collections to the furtherance of federal housing goals. Given control of federal resources now spent on housing, it is likely that state and local officials would not spend those resources to subsidize housing.

In a very broad sense, giving such control of federal spending to state and local officials and watching those resources be withdrawn from subsidized housing could be said to result in "savings."

UNCOMMITTED STATE RESOURCES

It is tempting to think that fiscal responsibilities devolved from the federal government to the states will find states with ample, otherwise uncommitted, resources that will be applied to covering the previous federal costs. This is simply wrong-headed thinking for several readily apparent reasons.

First, the states do not have uncommitted resources.[5] As discussed in Chapter Two, the costs of maintaining the services they already provide exceed likely revenues from the taxes and fees now in place. The scheduled decline in federal domestic discretionary spending will exacerbate this problem. So will future commitments state officials have already made, such as tax cuts to be phased in over periods of as long as ten years and multiyear programs to improve educational quality. So will the impacts of voter-initiated tax and spending limits. So will the impacts of state court decisions on school finance equalization. So will any new unfunded federal mandates emanating from the Congress, executive branch agencies, and federal courts.

Second, even if states did have uncommitted resources, there is no reason why state officials would find devolved federal programs to have a higher priority for use of those resources than alternative uses popular with state officials, such as cutting taxes and adding spending on law enforcement, economic development, and improving educational quality.

MONEY IS FUNGIBLE

Like oil, wheat, and similar commodities, money is *fungible*. Like quantities can be freely substituted for each other regardless of origin. As a result, life is full of examples illustrating that attempts to earmark cash are often futile because the recipient can use the cash for the designated purpose while freeing equal resources to be used for any purpose.

Grandmother's $20 gift for a child can be used to purchase a toy or article of clothing for the child that the family would have purchased anyhow. While grandmother can be thanked for that particular thing, the net effect is that the family has $20 more purchasing power to spend on anything it wants. Donors to the United Fund and similar umbrella charities can earmark their contributions, but the usual effect is to create equal and offsetting reductions in the amount the designated charity receives from funds that are not earmarked. Purchasers of tickets in state lotteries may correctly believe that lottery profits go to education, which in an accounting sense they do in most states. Those familiar with state finances recognize that the impact is usually to supplant spending that would otherwise be made with state general funds. So the economic effect of purchasing lottery tickets may be increased spending for Medicaid or prisons or even tax cuts, not spending for education.

The history of federal grant administration is replete with instances in which federal officials have attempted to ensure that federal funds "supplement, not supplant" state and local spending. Decades of experimentation with earmarking, accounting rules, nonsupplantation provisions, maintenance-of-effort requirements, and matching provisions have demonstrated that these efforts are largely futile.[6]

They become even more futile if flexibility in the use of federal funds is increased as part of devolution. To return to an earlier example, state officials given flexibility might decide that the most cost-effective way to attack drug abuse is by mental health services for drug abusers rather than traditional substance abuse programs. If states have this flexibility, there is no effective way to prevent substitution of federal resources for state mental health spending that would have otherwise been paid for with state tax dollars.

The fungible nature of federal money opens the door for states to redirect federal resources away from the stated purposes of broad-based federal aid. Offering states the opportunity to keep 100 percent of savings in devolved programs, a feature of welfare reform and many devolution proposals, invites them through that door. New flexibility in permitted uses of federal funds facilitates their passage. As a result, spending on federally aided programs that have been devolved becomes subject to the same competition for priorities in state spending as spending on programs states finance with their own resources.

REDUCED SPENDING ON DEVOLVED FUNCTIONS

Devolution that saves money in the federal budget will, if programs are continued without change, reduce the purchasing power of state governments, the *income effect* previously described. Devolution will also create a *substitution effect*.

Ending matching changes the effective price of state and local spending. Welfare reform provides an example. Before reform, spending an additional dollar on welfare cost states an average of forty-three cents. After reform, it cost a dollar.

Likewise, saving a dollar by spending less on welfare saved state budgets only forty-three cents before reform but now saves a dollar. From the purchaser's perspective, the price of welfare benefits has more than doubled—precisely, it has increased by 133 percent (a hundred compared with forty-three)—and the savings from not buying welfare have been comparably increased. Other things being equal, this should reduce spending on welfare relative to spending on other state and local functions for the same reasons that a 133 percent increase in the price of meat tends to cause less consumption of meat and more consumption of chicken and fish.

The substitution effect is even more powerful in situations where federal earmarking has been effective. Such situations arise primarily in narrow categorical programs, which offer states funds to pursue objectives of low or no priority to them, not in broad areas such as transportation, education, and health where earmarking is less effective because states can substitute federal resources for tax-supported spending. To take an example, assume a federal program designed to construct pyramids. Offered 100 percent federal funding, states are likely to participate. Indeed, they might well provide funds for low matching requirements, such as 10 percent, calculating that the economic development benefits of the resulting federal spending would justify such outlays. Under such a program, the price of building pyramids is artificially pegged at zero to ten cents on the dollar, and 90 percent to 100 percent of any savings from not building pyramids will revert to the federal government. If pyramid building is incorporated in a broader federal program or block grant under devolution, states will have the option to use federal funds for projects on which they would otherwise spend money, such as monuments and public works of other kinds. So, they will be able to use federal funds to supplant their own scheduled spending. This changes the price of pyramid building to a hundred cents on the dollar.

Both the income and the substitution effects of devolution will cause spending for devolved federal programs to drop. The income effect reduces the ability of state and local governments to spend on every program, including the devolved ones. The substitution effect makes the devolved programs more expensive in relation to benefits than before, while all other programs competing for state resources retain their former costs and benefits.

This conclusion is not surprising. The purpose of having federal aid programs earmarked to narrow categorical purposes, matching requirements, and rigid prescriptions and prohibitions in grant programs, is to get state governments to do things they would not otherwise do. To the extent these features of federal programs are reduced or eliminated, states should be expected to revert to what they would otherwise do.

Some critics of welfare reform and devolution of other programs for the poor claim devolution will cause a "race to the bottom" as states compete to reduce their safety net spending.[7] The argument ascribes different motivations to the predicted race—ranging from presumed insensitivity to the needs of the poor by state officials to presumed widespread fears of states becoming "welfare magnets."

Evidence from implementation of welfare reform to date does not support the prediction that such a race will occur. States have generally been increasing their per-case welfare spending. The debates over welfare reform measures in individual states have not produced the citation of welfare magnetism as a major problem except in special situations, such as concerns by Wisconsin officials about in-migration from Illinois. Instead of being interested in competing with other states to have low welfare payments, most state officials are interested in moving toward an objective of having no cash welfare recipients. Desires to achieve this objective are based on public opinion and views of appropriate social policies and government spending, not on competitive factors involving policies of other states.

INCREASED BENEFIT DISPARITIES

Variations among States: As shown in Chapter 2, state policies have led to wide disparities among states in social welfare programs and spending. Other things being equal, these disparities would be expected to increase with shifts of financial responsibilities to the states. Devolution increases the range of possible policy differences among states and heightens state sensitivity to the financial impacts of those differences.

The price effects described above will be largest in the states with the lowest per capita incomes, which already have the least generous safety net programs. For example, the former cash welfare and current Medicaid programs use federal matching percentages that vary inversely with state per capita incomes within a range between a minimum 50 percent federal match and a maximum 80 percent match in the poorest states. A shift to 100 percent state costs for benefit increases and 100 percent state benefits from savings will increase the costs of providing benefits in Mississippi fivefold, replacing programs available at twenty cents on the dollar by programs available only at a hundred cents on the dollar. The same shift will just double the incremental costs of benefits in more affluent Connecticut, replacing programs available at fifty cents on the dollar with programs available at a hundred cents on the dollar.

The income effects as they affect tax raising will be more pronounced in states with low fiscal capacity than in those with higher fiscal capacity. To replace a lost dollar of federal funds in West Virginia, for example, requires a 30 percent greater tax rate increase than in the average state, but a lower rate increase in New Jersey than in the average state.

So, the combination of price and income effects will likely increase the differentials in the provision of public services affected by devolution.

In addition to these effects, the increasing flexibility associated with devolution allows the states to differentiate their policies more from each other, as they have done with the "toughness" of their work requirements under welfare reform. In income maintenance programs some states are likely to pare benefits for some recipients (e.g., families without members with jobs) in order to increase benefits for other recipients (e.g., families with minimum-wage jobs) more than other states faced with the same options. In health programs, some states are likely to resolve trade-offs between prevention and treatment and between children and the elderly differently than other states.

Other things being equal, cuts in spending levels of devolved programs are more likely in states with weak fiscal positions than in fiscally strong states. Long-term, states with structural surpluses are less likely to cut benefits than states with structural deficits. Short-term, states with the largest fiscal dividends from rapid economic growth are less likely to cut benefits than those experiencing fiscal problems of slow growth and localized recession.

Other things being equal, cuts in spending levels of devolved programs are more likely in states whose elected officials have strong commitments to reducing tax burdens than in states where there is less concern with reducing taxes. Which states fall in which category varies with election results, but long-term pressures for tax reduction are greatest in states with aggregate tax burdens substantially higher than competing states. New York provides one current example.

An independent effect on benefit levels will occur with the devolution of any program that includes some sort of freezing of federal funding at a level based on past spending, as federal welfare reform did. Such freezes have quite uneven effects. They are not necessarily burdensome and may create windfalls, as welfare reform did, in states with demographic outlooks likely to reduce workloads. Most northeastern states provide examples for welfare, but other states would provide examples in transportation, education, and other programs.

Conversely, the burdens of rising costs will become most substantial in states with the reverse demographic situations. In the case of welfare reform, the examples are fast-growing Sunbelt states.

Variations within States: The rhetoric of devolution constantly includes phrases like "returning power to the states" and "shifting powers to the states." This correctly reflects the federal perspective that power over policy is being moved from Washington to the state capitols.

But the notion that discretion will be exercised on a state-by-state basis after devolution doesn't reflect the traditions, political realities, and policy preferences of elected officials in many of the states. There is a strong argument that a single cookie-cutter federal policy made in Washington cannot be appropriately applied to the diverse situations of rural farming areas, desert and mountain areas, the ghettos of large central cities, middle class suburbs, and so on.

These same arguments are nearly as salient when made against cookie-cutter policies made in state capitols such as in Albany, Austin, Springfield, Sacramento, and Tallahassee as they are when made against cookie-cutter policies emanating from Washington, D.C.

Particularly in the most populous states, there are long traditions and strong public policy arguments for relying heavily on policy control and some sharing of financing responsibilities by local governments. This can be seen in the implementation of welfare reform. Some large states have already delegated much of their authority over eligibility requirements and remedial programs to counties. The result will be a diversity of policies (and thus in the treatment of similarly situated households) within states as well as among states.

Proponents of decentralized decision-making will find this development a healthy signal, but not all Americans may react the same way to the resulting inconsistency in policies.

TAX LEVELS AND BURDENS

To the extent that state-financed spending is increased by devolution, the result must be higher state taxes than would otherwise exist. This result will inherently cause the nation's tax system to become more regressive as no state tax options are as progressive as the federal income tax.

SPENDING ON STATE PRIORITIES

To the extent that shifts of federal costs to states are neither offset by savings nor handled by increasing taxes, the costs must be covered by reductions in the amounts states would otherwise spend on non-devolved functions. Absent a basis for predicting any other result, such reductions would probably affect such spending roughly in the proportions of such spending in state and local budgets. This would suggest that the largest impacts would be felt in elementary and secondary education, followed by health care, followed by higher education.

CYCLICAL SENSITIVITY

Absent federal action to offset the effects, devolution of any program will sharply alter the likely change in benefits during recession. Lodged in the federal government, such programs are more likely to be expanded than contracted to deal with recession. Lodged in state and local governments, they are likely to share in budget cuts, as these governments strive to restore balanced budgets.

CONCLUSION

The consequences described in this chapter can be predicted with considerable confidence as inevitable results of devolution. Hopefully, this report has brought to readers' attention both facts and analytical insights supporting these predictions.

Appraisal of the "goodness" or "badness" of these consequences is quite another matter. Such appraisals depend upon many different value judgments on such matters as the relative importance of nationally uniform policies, appropriate roles for government in affecting the relative economic status of the rich and poor, and concepts of what governments should do and how much they should tax.

The fiscal effects described in this paper will alarm some readers. Increasing benefit disparities among states, cutting previous benefit levels, leaving the poor more subject to the ravages of recession than they already are, raising regressive taxes, and squeezing resources out of education and health care aren't good ideas to many observers. But there is another side to devolution not emphasized in this paper. A smaller and cheaper federal government, increased citizen control of policies, programs more tailored to local situations and priorities, more cost-effective administration and less paperwork, experimentation in fifty laboratories of democracy, and other claimed effects of devolution are good ideas to many observers.

The author would like to believe that his ability to understand and predict the fiscal consequences of devolution is superior to that of most readers. But he does not claim equal superiority in comparing the administrative competence, much less the compassion, of state and federal officials. He brings no special competence to making value judgments necessary to conclude whether, all things considered, devolution represents the best direction for national policy.

APPENDIX A

DEVOLUTION:
STATUS AND PENDING CHANGES

POSSIBLE PATTERNS FOR DEVOLUTION

The possibilities for devolution are best understood by a matrix reflecting possible changes in federal funding separately from possible changes in federal policy control. The range of possible outcomes resulting from changes in funding or mandates is represented in Figure A.1.

FIGURE A.1

	Federal Funding Increased	Federal Funding Constant	Federal Funding Reduced
Federal Mandates Increased	Centralization	Unfunded Mandates	Worst Case Scenario
Federal Mandates Constant	Fiscal Relief	Status Quo	Shift and Shaft
Federal Mandates Reduced	Fiscal Windfall	Block Grants	Pure Devolution

For any particular program (e.g., special education), function (e.g., elementary and secondary education), and for overall federal interaction with state and local governments, there is a status quo. It reflects the current level of federal funding and current federal controls over policy and administration. Projected into the future, it assumes no changes in federal controls and only the changes in funding required to maintain existing policies. Specifically, it assumes that funding will increase in response to changes in price levels (inflation) and to changes in underlying workloads, such as the number of children to be educated. The matrix reflects the possibilities that federal control and federal funding can be altered independently.

Symmetrical Changes

If policy controls and funding were linked, the two would change symmetrically only by increases in both or by decreases in both (see Figure A.2).

Pure Devolution: Symmetrical reductions in federal control and federal funding have historically been more discussed than implemented. Historical examples can be found almost exclusively among relatively tiny federal grant programs that have been eliminated. For example, the federal government once maintained a separate categorical program for rat control.

Figure A.2

	Federal Funding Increased	Federal Funding Constant	Federal Funding Reduced
Federal Mandates Increased	Centralization		
Federal Mandates Constant		Status Quo	
Federal Mandates Reduced			Pure Devolution

The best current example of a proposal for pure devolution has come out of frustrations associated with federal highway programs. While recognizing the desirability of federal control and funding of highways integral to movement among states, typified by the Interstate Highway System, many observers have questioned the rationale for federal control of roads of purely local significance, such as local streets and arterial roads and rural farm-to-market roads.

Federal involvement in such local projects unquestionably lengthens the time between decisions to improve capacity and completion of construction. It also increases costs by requiring design standards sometimes in excess of what local officials would prefer and by setting conditions attached to uses of federal funds associated with relocation, mitigation of environmental impacts, paying prevailing wages, minority contractor preferences, and more. Dissatisfaction is particularly high in states that do not receive federal road funds proportional to what their highway users pay in federal gasoline and diesel fuel taxes.

The proffered solution is often referred to as a "turn-back" of responsibilities and tax sources to state and local government. It would involve eliminating the portion of federal gasoline taxes and other highway user charges associated with the targeted federal programs. Those programs and all of the mandates associated with them would be eliminated. While popular with some transportation officials and some members of Congress, the concept has not appealed to most state and local elected officials. To them, it means their taking responsibility for raising state and local taxes merely to provide for activities at current levels. Recognizing that state and local officials might not raise taxes enough to equal the repealed federal taxes, some transportation interest groups also fear a likely reduction in total spending on highways.

Centralization: There are many examples of simultaneous federal assumption of responsibilities for financing and policy control. One of the most significant was federal acceptance of responsibility for the cash assistance needs of the aged, blind, and disabled under the Supplemental Security Income (SSI) program adopted in the 1970s. Previous state and local assistance programs with varying benefits and different eligibility conditions were replaced by a uniform definition of eligibility and nationally uniform payments. State and local governments had no obligations. They had the opportunity to retain

their staffs as contractors for the federal government, which they generally did. They had the opportunity to add to the federal payments,
which about half the states did.

Less pure examples of centralization appear periodically in new
federal grant programs. The child health initiative included as part of
the federal budget legislation enacted in 1997 is an example. The federal government established a new program targeted at uninsured children in low and moderate income households, set minimum standards
for state programs but allowed considerable state flexibility in implementation, and offered federal funding for more than half of the costs.

INCREASING FEDERAL CONTROL WITHOUT PROPORTIONATE FUNDING

The matrix in Figure A.3 shows three possibilities involving increased
federal control over state and local policy without increases in federal funding.

Unfunded Mandates: State and local officials constantly complain
about federal directives (mandates) that raise their costs but are unac-
companied by compensating increases in federal aid (unfunded). No
devolution is involved when federal officials add unfunded mandates,

FIGURE A.3

	Federal Funding Increased	Federal Funding Constant	Federal Funding Reduced
Federal Mandates Increased		Unfunded Mandates	Worst Case Scenario
Federal Mandates Constant		Status Quo	Shift and Shaft
Federal Mandates Reduced			

but devolution increases the vulnerability of state and local finances to future unfunded mandates. With no federal sharing of costs, mandates become an even cheaper alternative for federal officials than when costs are shared.

Shift and Shaft: State and local officials live in constant fear that the federal government will retain present mandates but reduce its funding associated with those mandates. The fiscally most significant example comes from recurring proposals to cap the growth in federal outlays for low-income health care provided under Medicaid. With no other changes, such a policy simply results in shifting cost burdens.

Worst Case Scenario: The worst case scenario, from a state and local perspective, would arise if the federal government were simultaneously to increase what it requires from state and local governments through mandates while reducing its cost-sharing through federal budget cuts.

INCREASING FEDERAL FUNDING WITHOUT CONTROL INCREASES

The matrix in Figure A.4 shows three possibilities involving increased federal funding without increases in federal control over state and local policy.

FIGURE A.4

	Federal Funding Increased	Federal Funding Constant	Federal Funding Reduced
Federal Mandates Increased			
Federal Mandates Constant	Fiscal Relief	Status Quo	
Federal Mandates Reduced	Fiscal Windfall	Block Grants	

Fiscal Relief: Increases in federal funds without changes in federal control cannot be viewed as devolution. But such increases illustrate the possibility of federal policy changes that could offset adverse fiscal effects of devolution by increases in funding for unrelated programs. One recent example is the package of tax expenditures for higher education that passed the Congress as part of the budget agreement of 1997. By a combination of new deductions and tax credits available to individual taxpayers, federal action has decreased the after-tax costs of tuition paid to state universities and community colleges. This gives state governments more flexibility to raise revenues by tuition increases.

Also in the budget agreement, Congress agreed that the 4.3 cents of federal gasoline tax revenues previously going for general federal purposes would be earmarked for highways. Although not self-executing, the change is likely to lead to increases in federal highway aid with no shift in the present patterns of federal controls.

Block Grants: The concept of block grants won support from most state and local officials and some federal officials long before the current discussion of devolution. The idea is that program effectiveness would be improved if narrow categorical programs were consolidated into a small number of broader programs. Rather than forcing state and local officials into narrow choices—such as how to spend federal computer or teacher training money—block grants would allow them to optimize choices to attain a broad objective, such as better schools. Most current discussion of block grants occurs in the context of constant federal funding, but the concept is appropriate for any given level of funding, whether higher, constant, or lower. In 1995 much of the discussion of block grants was in the context of reduced funding. The concept was that more efficient use of funds through block grants would make it possible for state and local governments to handle reduced federal funding without reducing services.

Fiscal Windfalls: Producing windfalls for state and local government by simultaneously increasing federal funding and decreasing federal controls has never been described as an objective of federal devolution policy. However, the prime recent example of devolution, welfare reform, clearly produces such windfalls—at least in the first two years of implementation. The program guaranteed each state the funding levels of a base year. Because the amounts guaranteed turned out to be greater than aid that would have been provided under the old matching program, nearly all states received more in money from the new program than they would have from the old.

Some windfalls are inherently a part of federal actions that preclude further increases or cuts in total funding and/or pay for actions previously funded by some states. In such circumstances, it is almost impossible to design a program that doesn't provide windfall revenue for a few states. Also, block grants usually involve changing distribution formulas in some fashion. In practice, it is difficult for legislative bodies to pass such new formulas without holding losers harmless, at least for an initial year or two, while providing some increases for winners.

DEVOLUTION AND PREEMPTION

Although the terminology is used somewhat loosely, federal "mandate" is a term used to describe directives to state and local government, normally in connection with a promise of federal aid or a threat to cut off aid under an existing program if mandates are not accepted. On the other hand, "preemption" refers to federal actions that preclude states from exercising legal powers that states held prior to the federal action. For example, federal legislation is under consideration that would preempt state powers to tax commerce arising on the Internet. Recent federal determinations to regulate forms of private health insurance preempt previous state legislation on the subject, as would proposed federal tobacco settlement legislation, which would preempt state laws on subjects ranging from tort law to control of smoking in public buildings.

DEVOLUTION AND FEDERAL COURTS

Issues of devolution are usually discussed as though all the relevant federal decisions were being made by the president and the Congress. However, some of the federal actions that most significantly affect state and local finances occur in federal courtrooms. The portions of these actions that interpret federal statutes are subject to change by legislation, but those interpreting the U.S. Constitution are not. Examples of the latter include decisions requiring outlays by states and school districts for desegregation remedies, such as busing and magnet schools, and for the improvement of conditions in prisons and jails, such as how much cell space is provided to each prisoner.

THE NEAR-TERM OUTLOOK FOR DEVOLUTION

The federal budget compromises of 1997 arguably set the course for the future of devolution at least through 1998. They leave uncertainties primarily over two subjects: (1) potential future cuts in federal grants to state and local governments and (2) federal mandates and preemption not directly associated with grant programs.

Funding Uncertainties: The compromise budget legislation promises to achieve a balanced federal budget by 2002. For this to be achieved under the plan, there must be a systematic reduction in the purchasing power of federal funds for "domestic discretionary" spending. While such cuts were assumed in the compromise, the details of such reductions were never specified and thus not debated.

The domestic discretionary category consists of the operations of many federal agencies and programs and most grants to state and local governments other than those associated with entitlement programs, particularly Medicaid. Even if grants were cut only proportionally to their share of the total category, substantial reductions in their purchasing power would be required to implement the budget agreement. If other portions of the category—such as funds for the operation of Congress itself—prove impervious to reductions, grant reductions will have to be disproportionate.

The planned reductions are timed so that they do not involve politically hazardous decisions on education, transportation, and other programs until after the 1998 elections. The budget agreement also included funding increases before then for many of the programs that need to be an object of reductions thereafter. Many observers are skeptical that the president and the Congress taking office in 1999 will in fact make these reductions.

Federal Control Uncertainties: The compromise is also silent on the issue of decisions affecting state and local finances other than through federal grants. Many such decisions are embodied in legislation now under consideration. Some may be enacted before 1999. Many examples involve adverse impacts on state and local finances and/or sharp reductions in state and local powers currently being exercised. More such measures on unpredictable topics are likely to be discussed seriously over the next several years.

By no means do all of the federal policies under serious consideration involve adverse impacts on state and local finances. Some entail significant increases in federal outlays, which would provide fiscal relief for state and local governments. The most prominent current example is the recently enacted highway financing legislation.

DEVOLUTION ISSUES NOW PENDING

The debates of 1995 through 1997 resulted in a budget resolution that sets the course of federal funding through 2002 and passage of several important measures affecting federalism, particularly welfare reform legislation and legislation making it more difficult to enact unfunded mandates. While there will likely be disputes around the edges of those policies, barring massive changes in the nation's circumstances, these compromises appear likely to govern federal policies through the elections of 1998. But there are possible exceptions and many issues to be decided within this basic framework. Using the decisions of 1996 and 1997 as a baseline, the paragraphs below discuss these exceptions and issues.

Elementary and Secondary Education: Federal funding and controls would not change under the new budget agreement. Some members of Congress are pushing for broad block grants that would substantially increase state and local flexibility while other members are pushing new categorical programs (e.g., to promote school choice), additional earmarking of funds, and further restrictions associated with current categorical programs. Federal roles in standard setting are being debated primarily in connection with proposals for national achievement tests, which are likely not to be mandatory as in the legislation currently being debated.

Higher Education: The budget legislation of 1997 saw a sharp expansion of the federal role in financing community college and university education. The mechanism chosen was tax expenditures (use of targeted tax reductions to achieve results that might otherwise be achieved by spending). This approach is not intrusive on state and local control but will provide indirect fiscal relief because it reduces the after-tax costs—to the student and the student's financial sponsors—of tuition at public institutions. The legislation provides tax credits for tuition payments in grades 13 and 14, new deductions for tuition payments, increases flexibility and improves tax treatment of state prepaid tuition plans, and establishes new tax benefits for savings ultimately used to pay tuition. No significant increases in federal controls are inherent in these measures.

Consistent with this federal choice for applying additional federal resources through subsidizing the customer/student rather than the producer/university, subsequent federal budgets are likely to continue a trend to reduce direct subsidies to universities. Those subsidies are a small factor in total higher education finance and are mostly confined to special situations such as medical education and historically black colleges.

Health Care: Little change is contemplated in federal impacts on state-administered public health and mental health programs. Considerable expansion of the federal role in the traditionally state field of the regulation of health care providers and health care insurance is underway in legislation affecting the services that must be offered by providers (e.g., overnight stays for maternity cases) and arrangements between patients and providers (e.g., prohibiting physicians from participating in Medicare if they assess charges to any Medicare patient in excess of the Medicare reimbursement).

Low-income health care will continue to be provided through the Medicaid program, with peripheral changes. Some of those changes, such as repeal of federal provisions affecting reimbursement rates for health care providers, enhance state and local flexibility. The federal role in financing health care of low-income children is being expanded through a new grant program. Proposals to convert Medicaid to block grants appear dead.

Income Maintenance: Welfare reform legislation was adopted in 1996 and is now being implemented, with few changes likely to affect cash assistance under the former AFDC program. In broad outline, welfare reform eliminates federal assistance under some circumstances (such as families exceeding time limits for being on welfare or refusing work requirements) while providing immensely more flexibility to states to design and administer welfare cash assistance and other programs that provide and subsidize work alternatives to welfare.

Child Support Enforcement: Previously existing state systems associated with the establishment of paternal status and obligations to support children of unwed and divorced parents are gradually being replaced through establishment of a national system including uniform national guidelines for child support enforcement and a nationwide information system.

Children's Programs: In addition to the programs listed above, the federal government has many impacts on programs affecting children. Federal support of preschool activities (e.g., Headstart) appears likely to continue. Rules affecting foster care and adoption are being altered, with the outcome in terms of increasing or decreasing federal controls unclear. Much the same situation prevails in day care, with advocates of new federal standards and categorical grant programs pressing their case at the same time that state officials have new flexibility under the welfare reform legislation to provide day care by nontraditional means such as through grandparents and neighbors providing care.

Job Training and Placement Programs: Legislation to consolidate the many federal programs that provide job training appears to be widely favored by federal and state and local elected officials, but has produced substantial opposition from a variety of other interests. It was finally enacted in late 1998.

Law Enforcement: Crime was the number-one voter concern shown by most polls taken during the early and mid-1990s, leading to much more extensive federal involvement in the field. The results have included a major new grant program in support of law enforcement, extensive new federal anticrime activities overlapping state and local criminal laws and enforcement, and a variety of federal actions preempting or requiring changes to state laws. Examples are gun control and the prohibition against weapons carrying by law enforcement officials with records of domestic violence. There is no significant effort to reduce federal roles in law enforcement and many proposals to increase them.

As is the case with other grant programs falling in the federal "domestic discretionary" category, future funding of current federal law enforcement grants is in doubt.

Water and Sewer: Federal legislation has been on the books for several decades allowing federal regulation of local water supply. This legislation was recently revised to somewhat reduce mandates and costs viewed as extreme but also to reaffirm federal intentions to apply national standards to water supply for household use. Federal water pollution control laws have been on the books for decades to require minimum standards for sewer systems (e.g., separation of storm and sanitary systems) and sewage treatment processes. The original legislation contemplated that federal funds would cover about half the costs of compliance, but federal funding levels have been essentially frozen for nearly a decade, leaving state and local governments with most of the costs of compliance, which are measurable in hundreds of billions of dollars. No significant moves are underway to shift either the funding or the regulatory framework of federal activities in these fields.

Solid Waste: Because of concerns with water pollution, air pollution, and energy conservation through recycling, the federal government has established a framework of control over solid waste disposal throughout the nation. Although the original regulatory framework was enacted with substantial federal grant support of mandated outlays, that grant support has been trivial in relation to mandated costs. Huge outlays have been made for landfills and resource recovery operations and much more would be required to implement the original objectives of federal regulators. Recently federal officials have backed away from some of the mandates for reasons unrelated to devolution policies in general. The specific motivating factors have been: (1) adverse-to-hostile reactions to state and local officials over the mandates and the costs of complying with them and (2) changes in the perceptions by experts in the field of the magnitude of the problems and the appropriate solutions.

Highways and Streets: There has been little change in the basic funding logic and degree of federal control in the years since the passage of the federal authorizing legislation currently governing highway spending. That legislation expired in late 1997, giving rise to a range of proposed changes. On one extreme there were proposals to turn back some programs to the states and eliminate an associated portion of the federal gasoline tax. On the other was a plan to authorize a new system of federally aided highways—a successor to the Interstate System that would identify additional highways as equivalent to the national status of the Interstates.

Funding promised to be the first major challenge to the ceilings on domestic spending of the congressional budget compromise of 1997. Having failed to achieve increased federal spending during the budget process, transportation interests (including many state and local officials) successfully obtained a shift of 4.3 cents of federal gasoline tax revenues from the federal general fund to the federal highway trust fund. This change in trust fund revenue doesn't automatically increase federal highway spending (which inherently mostly takes the form of grants to state and local governments) but strengthens the case for it.

Various proposals have been made in connection with the reauthorization legislation that suggest the contradictory approaches to devolution that can appear side-by-side in federal legislation affecting billions of dollars annually and reaching into every state and congressional district. Some, such as additional congressional earmarking of federal money to specific projects violating the priorities of state highway agencies, were distinctly not devolution. Some, such as allowing somewhat more flexibility to state and local officials in planning and construction of local roads, moved in a devolutionary direction.

Mass Transit: Besides illustrating many of the same issues associated with reauthorization of federal highway legislation, which includes transit, the recent history of transit funding and policy control suggests a good example of withdrawal of federal funding without major changes in federal control. Over the past ten years, federal budget pressures and criticisms of unequal distribution (among other factors) have caused elected officials of both parties to favor reduced federal support of the operating costs of transit, which can be seen in the amounts and patterns of federal aid. Major aspects of federal mandates, such as many controls over local labor-management relations, remain and will likely continue to do so as a condition of receiving federal assistance in capital costs, even if federal assistance ends for operating costs.

Regulation: Some regulatory issues and mandates are associated with the federal budget process. That is, the issues are considered by the same committees handling the budget with either sole or shared jurisdiction, and are resolved in the context of federal budget compromises. Other regulatory issues proceed on different tracks, independent of the budget process. Such legislation travels a different track in the federal process because it has little or no link to federal spending. But it may have substantial links to state and local spending or revenue raising. Federal unfunded mandates legislation was designed to require Congress to take these impacts into account by subjecting proposals involving mandates to processes requiring, among other things, calculation of their fiscal effects on state and local government. It is too early to appraise how significant the new procedures will prove to be.

Federal legislation dealing only with regulatory matters has shown little sign of the interest in devolution associated with federal legislation on the budget track. For example, highly preemptive provisions are found in legislation being seriously considered or enacted and dealing with such subjects as taxation of the Internet, regulation of health care providers, regulation and deregulation of cable TV, resolution of tobacco-related issues, and deregulation of the electric utility industry.

Appendix B

Characteristics of State and Local Finances

State and Local Finances and Programs Intertwined

This report deals with the finances of state and local government on a combined basis because the finances of these two levels of government are closely intertwined in every state. Much of what most states do financially is to collect money from their citizens and give it to local officials who, in turn, spend it for public services. For example, states finance nearly half of all public school costs. Large portions of local road construction and maintenance costs in most states come from revenues the state collects from gasoline taxes and vehicle registration fees.

The patterns of state and local fiscal interactions differ considerably among the states. For example, schools are a function of local governments in forty-nine states, but are run by the state in Hawaii. Roads are a local function in most states, but are built and maintained by the state in Delaware. Most states pay almost the entire cost of welfare, but many states including California require local governments to foot much of the bill for cash assistance to families and individuals without children. Nearly every state pays the costs of low-income health care under Medicaid, but New York requires a large local contribution. Local governments run charity hospitals, but some states don't have any government-run charity hospitals and in Louisiana they are run by the state.

For many years, the federal government provided much of its grant assistance directly to local governments. However, much to the dismay of some local officials, this pattern has gradually been shifting toward providing most aid directly to state governments and giving state officials substantial control over the sub-state distributions and uses of much of the rest. One reason for the shift has been program-by-program decisions by federal officials to stress state roles. Another has been decades of massive changes in where Americans live, resulting in smaller percentages of people in large local governments, such as central cities, and larger percentages receiving services from smaller municipalities, counties, and townships. Yet another has been the change in the mix of federal assistance. A constantly rising percentage of federal grant spending has been directed to entitlement programs, such as welfare and Medicaid, which are predominately managed by states. A declining percentage has been associated with local roads, wastewater treatment, and other functions where the local role is predominant.

THE FEDERAL ROLE IN STATE AND LOCAL FINANCES

In the data compiled by the Census Bureau FY 1994 federal aid accounted for approximately 23 percent of state and local general revenue.[1] Federal aid provides more revenue to state and local governments than any single tax source, such as property taxes or sales taxes.

Federal aid has effects on state and local finances that vary with the type of assistance provided. At one extreme, federal aid primarily substitutes for money that would otherwise be raised by local governments and states. For example, if there were no federal support of construction of arterial streets in urban areas, state and local funds would likely be used to maintain about the same level of construction. At the other extreme, federal aid supplements state and local funding, adding to whatever these governments would otherwise spend. Federal support of special programs for disadvantaged public school students is an example. The largest federal outlays are in matching programs, which combine federal and state and local funds in fixed ratios. The entire Medicaid program and Interstate Highways are examples.

TRENDS IN SPENDING AND TAXES

Levels: State and local government taxes take about 11 percent of the nation's personal income. This percentage has been relatively stable for several decades.

State and local spending has been rising as a percentage of personal income as a result of two forms of financing spending other than by taxes: (1) federal aid, which has been growing faster than personal income and state and local tax revenues and (2) non-tax revenues such as those associated with user charges, for example, university tuition and water and sewer charges.

Composition: Certain tax revenues are traditionally earmarked for particular spending, such as gasoline taxes used to construct and maintain highways and Unemployment Compensation payroll taxes used to pay benefits to the unemployed. Excluding them, about a third of state and local revenues come from property taxes, about a third from sales and excise taxes, and 22 percent from personal income taxes. The rest comes from a variety of other sources, the largest of which is taxes on corporate income, which raise just under 5 percent of all state and local tax revenues.

Through about 1990, there was a systematic nationwide trend toward lower reliance on local taxes, particularly the property tax, and increased reliance on state taxes, particularly income and sales taxes. Since the early 1990s, both the percentage of state and local tax revenues raised by states and the composition of tax revenues has remained relatively stable.

Considering spending on a basis comparable to most state and local budgets,[2] just over 26 percent of all state and local spending is associated with public schools. The next largest category, at 12.4 percent, is the Medicaid program's support of the health care costs of low-income beneficiaries. The third largest single category is higher education, with just under 6 percent of the total.

The past decade has seen significant shifts in state and local spending priorities. Medicaid and to a lesser degree corrections (prisons and jails) have claimed larger portions of state and local spending, squeezing down the percentage of total spending on education and other functions.

NOTES

1

1. These preferences consistently appeared in the surveys of the U.S. Advisory Commission on Intergovernmental Relations published as *Changing Attitudes on Spending and Taxes* before the commission was abolished. Similar preferences appear in periodic opinion surveys in individual states.

2. In federal discussions and in this paper, devolution is discussed as though it reflects a transfer of power from the federal government to state governments. It is important to understand that states are unlikely to keep many powers shifted from the federal government. Instead, each will, consistent with its own traditions and the preferences of its citizens, shift such power to local governments. This has already happened with welfare reform. Some states have delegated to counties the responsibility for decisions on benefit levels, eligibility, and the selection of alternative approaches to move welfare recipients into jobs. Rather than constantly using the phrase "state and local governments," this paper uses phrases like "the states" and "state governments."

2

1. For examples of the literature, see Stephen Mark, Therese McGuire, and Leslie Papke, "What Do We Know About the Effect of Taxes on Economic Development?" prepared for the District of Columbia Tax Revision Commission (reprinted in *State Tax Notes* [August 25, 1997]). Similar reviews of national literature summarized

from the perspectives of individual states are constantly being done for legislative committees and private groups with a stake in individual state outcomes. An example is *Review of Research on the Role of Taxes and Education in Explaining Economic Development and Growth,* prepared by Michael Bell and Murray Johnston (Baltimore: Johns Hopkins University, 1996) as part of the debate on whether to lower Maryland's personal income tax. Also see Peter Fisher and Alan Peters, "Tax and Spending Incentives and Enterprise Zones," *New England Economic Review* (March-April 1997): 109–38, reprinted in *State Tax Notes* (June 30, 1997); and Michael Wasylenko, "Taxation and Economic Development: the State of the Economic Literature," from the *New England Economic Review* (March-April 1997): 37–52, reprinted in *State Tax Notes* (June 23, 1997).

2. For a sample of studies connecting high taxes and slow economic growth, see Zsolt Becsi, "Do State and Local Taxes Affect Relative State Growth?" Federal Reserve Bank of Atlanta, *Economic Review* 81, no. 2 (March/April 1996): 18–36. For a review see Robert G. Lynch, "The Effectiveness of State and Local Tax Cuts and Incentives: A Review of the Literature," *State Tax Notes* (September 30, 1996). *State Policy Reports* (the twice-monthly newsletter on state policy written by the author of this paper) frequently compares such results to the close correlation between frequency of doctor visits and early mortality. The correlation is clear but the causal linkage is not.

3. The provisions of the welfare reform legislation allowing lower benefits for new migrants are being challenged in federal courts on the grounds that differentials violate "right to travel" guarantees of the U.S. Constitution. If they do, then state-imposed differences and congressional action approving such differences are invalid.

4. The discussion of structural deficits summarizes research by the author soon to be published, with revisions and updates, in "The Outlook for State and Local Finances: The Dangers of Structural Deficits to the Future of American Education," National Education Association Research Division, Washington, D.C., 1998.

5. Ronald Snell, ed., *Financing State Government in the 1990s,* (Washington, D.C.: National Conference of State Legislators, 1993).

6. The compromise does not include specific projections for grants to state and local government included within the broad category of federal domestic discretionary spending. However, the implication of scheduled cuts in the broad category is that grants within it are unlikely to grow as rapidly as would be required either to maintain

a constant percentage of personal income or to provide federal spending increases consistent with price increases and workload changes.

7. The specific growth reflected in the table reflects the author's estimate of the likely effect on grants of implementing the budget compromise. The assumed personal income growth reflects the assumptions underlying the federal budget compromise negotiations early in 1997. For updates, see note 6.

8. For a complete description of ways of measuring fiscal capacity and the results of each measure for each state, see *State Policy Reports* 2, vol. 16 (1998).

9. The methodology for such comparisons is well known among experts and widely accepted. However, it is tedious and expensive to apply. The Advisory Commission on Intergovernmental Relations historically did this work but stopped with the 1991 calculations. The commission no longer exists and no one has stepped forward to do the work until recently. A new report, based on the FY 1994 Census data on state and local finances, was recently published in Robert Tannenwald, *Come the Devolution Will States Be Able to Respond?* (Boston: Federal Reserve Bank of Boston, 1997).

10. The calculation of spending needs is roughly comparable to the calculation using FY 1991 data appearing in *State Policy Reports* 13, no. 20 (1995), which appears as Table G-21 in *State Fact Finder: Rankings Across America* (Washington, D.C.: Congressional Quarterly Press, various years). The new tables were developed by *State Policy Reports* using demographic and other workload data collected by Tannenwald as they appear in the technical appendix to his paper. For additional discussion of methodology and results, see *State Policy Reports* (16:5 [1998]). There is a significant difference between the assessment of spending needs in this report and that appearing in Tannenwald's study. The latter allows assumed needs for differentials in public worker compensation. Because over 70 percent of spending on major functions, such as education and law enforcement, is associated with employee compensation costs, such adjustments have a massive impact on the results. For example, Tannenwald concludes that New Jersey needs to pay its employees 20.9 percent more than the national average, 20.1 percent more than neighboring Delaware, 19.7 percent more than neighboring Pennsylvania, and 65 percent more than Montana and South Dakota. Periodic analyses by *State Policy Reports* conclude that such huge differences in what different states need to pay to recruit and retain qualified government employees do not exist, except in the case of

certain differences in Alaska and Hawaii. Besides being false, the assumed differences lead to circular reasoning, which can have major effects on state policies. Costs are presumed to be high because state and local taxes are high and state and local taxes must be high because the costs of government are high.

11. The Fiscal Comfort Index was first developed by the Advisory Commission on Intergovernmental Relations in a study published in 1990.

12. The comparisons of Medicaid spending come from "Variations in Medicaid Spending among States," policy brief A-3 in the series *Assessing New Federalism: Issues and Options for States*, (Washington, D.C.: Urban Institute, 1998); the comparisons on general assistance came from "General Assistance Programs: The State-Based Part of the Safety Net," policy brief A-4 in the same series (1998). All other comparisons come from *State Fact Finder*, various years.

13. In legal terms and in common usage, "state action" and "state policy" can be considered as any decision made by a state using whatever mechanisms it chooses to make those decisions. Federal mandates can follow this approach with impunity. The eligibility of a state for federal highway funds can be conditioned on adoption of particular policies on such subjects as speed limits, reimbursements to landowners for land taken for highway construction, limitations on billboards on private land, and use of preferences for minority contractors. If a state chooses not to comply with such mandates, it doesn't receive the federal money conditioned on compliance with the mandate. Mandates taking the form of regulation applied to state and local government—such as laws applicable to labor relations (e.g., minimum wage provisions) and to pollution control—are, in the words of the U.S. Constitution, the supreme law of the land. From this federal perspective, it makes no difference how a state happens to have made its policies or what procedures it uses to change them. Conflicting state laws must give way to the exercise of federal power. This is true in the normal case of state laws passed by legislatures and signed by governors. It is also true even if the state law is embodied in a state constitution, true if the state law was developed by decision of state courts, and true if the state law was established by voters themselves. With federal control supreme, different institutional arrangements for establishing state policy simply don't matter.

14. If a recession were to find states with balances in general funds and rainy day funds that are much higher than normal, part of the

response to recession would be to spend down these balances, which would be as countercyclical as the deficit spending of the federal government. If a recession were to occur in late 1997 or early 1998, it would find these balances at unusually high levels. However, large and unexpected surpluses from prior-year operations create strong temptations to increase spending and cut taxes, a factor that will likely have major effects on legislative fiscal actions in 1998 when the economic pressures are augmented by awareness that statewide elections will be held in most states in November of 1998. A recession starting about then would be similar to the situation in 1982, when state actions were clearly procyclical. If budget deficits can change total spending, by American businesses and consumers as well as by the government, they will affect spending on foreign goods as well as on domestic goods and thus have an impact on the trade deficit. If they influence output and economic growth, they will help determine contributions to, and hence the alleged future deficits in, the Social Security trust funds. They will also affect the resources available to support the nonworking elderly.

If trade deficits permit more domestic consumption and investment, they also increase the wherewithal to support the elderly. If they contribute to unemployment and reduce domestic output, they will increase budget deficits.

3

1. Various definitions of devolution are discussed in Chapter One. The discussion is amplified in a more rigorous fashion in Appendix A.

2. John Donahue, *Disunited States* (New York: Basic Books, 1997), collects economic and noneconomic criticisms of devolution and contains extensive citations to others.

3. Under the "Boren Amendment," which was removed from Medicaid legislation in 1997, health care providers had the option of seeking judicial determinations of reasonable rates. A variety of rules governing Medicaid have the effect of protecting certain vendors, such as publicly supported clinics.

4. The relocation provisions are typical of the impacts of many federal policies on state and local costs. A government buying property has the same duty to the tenants as a private buyer would have.

So if a tenant, such as a renter of an apartment or a store in a shopping center, has a month remaining on a lease, the buyer is obligated to honor the right to occupy for an additional month but is not obligated to pay for tenant moving costs. Uniform federal relocation policies require payments to the tenant in such situations.

5. Because most state finances are not managed smoothly over business cycles, state finances tend to gyrate between appearing in crisis and appearing flush. This report happens to be appearing in 1998 after a record-setting period of uninterrupted national prosperity, which has left many states with larger balances than usual. Some readers may see the report at a later time, when recession has left states with potential deficits and forced layoffs and across-the-board budget cuts. Neither temporary prosperity nor temporary adversity are indicative of state fiscal situations over longer periods.

6. Matching requirements alone have clearly failed as demonstrated by subsequent decisions to cap former Title XX (social service) outlays and widespread use of Medicaid funds to support previously existing outlays for state institutions for the disabled, charity hospitals, and school health programs. Failures with non-supplantation and maintenance-of-effort provisions are constantly documented in General Accounting Office reports on specific programs. The experience with passage and implementation of welfare reform illustrates likely outcomes with devolution. Proponents avoided any such requirements in their original legislative proposals. Objections that states would divert federal block grant funds resulted in compromises in the federal legislation that seek to avoid this possibility. A year after passage, prevailing estimates suggested states had converted one to two billion dollars to support of spending outside of welfare.

7. The case that competition will accelerate a race to the bottom, already under way for other reasons, appears in the congressional debates on welfare reform and in Donahue, *Disunited States*.

APPENDIX B

1. The percentage calculations derived from Census data reflect the author's adjustment of those data to make them conform more closely to state and local budget concepts. For example, patient revenues

of hospitals are included in the Census totals but excluded in those shown in this paper.

2. The distribution of spending reflects adjustments comparable to those described in the note above. For example, spending on higher education excludes amounts financed by tuition and spending on health excludes amounts financed by patient charges.

INDEX

About the Author

Harold A. Hovey began his career by working in the Office of the Secretary of Defense and Office of Management and Budget, but left federal service three decades ago. Since then, he has served as finance director of Ohio, budget director of Illinois, and staff director of a state reorganization commission in Connecticut. He has dealt day-to-day with federalism issues as a senior economist for the National Governors' Association and in consulting assignments for, among others, the Congressional Budget Office; the General Accounting Office; the House Budget Committee; the Office of Management and Budget; the Advisory Commission on Intergovernmental Relations; the Departments of Education, Health and Human Services, Transportation, and Treasury; the National Conference of State Legislatures; the Council of State Governments; the National Association of Counties; and the National League of Cities.

He is the president of State Policy Research, Inc. and the editor of its two major newsletters, *State Policy Reports* and *State Budget and Tax News*. State Policy Research also produces the statistical comparisons of the fifty states, *State Fact Finder: Rankings Across America,* published annually by Congressional Quarterly Press, as well as the *Sourcebook,* published each January as a statistical supplement to *Governing* magazine. He is the author of two books, many book chapters, and numerous articles. He has taught public finance and other topics in economics and public administration at Ohio State University.